LAW AND PROFES
IN NURSING
Second Edition

Withdrawn

LAW AND PROFESSIONAL CONDUCT IN NURSING

Second Edition

Ann P. Young BA, RGN, RNT, FRSH, Deputy Registrar, Nightingale and Guy's College of Health, London.

SCUTARI PRESS
London

A division of Scutari Projects, the publishing company of the Royal College of Nursing

First edition 1991
This edition first published 1994

British Library Cataloguing in Publication Data
Young, Ann P.
  Law and Professional Conduct in Nursing.
  – 2Rev.ed
  I. Title
  344.204414

  ISBN 1–871364–95–7

Phototypeset by Intype, London
Printed by Bell and Bain Ltd., Glasgow

Contents

Preface

Nurses are becoming increasingly concerned at the effect of the law on their work, whether it is assisting the police by writing statements, being sued for negligence in the civil courts or acting as witnesses in the coroners' courts. However, registered nurses are also very aware of the influence that the United Kingdom Central Council's Code of Professional Conduct has on their actions, both professionally and ethically. What was not immediately obvious when the Code was first published was that it also has legal implications and the ethical concepts of duty, responsibility, value of the individual and fair treatment are also legal concepts.

The aim of this book is to ensure that nurses understand the legal implications of the Code of Professional Conduct, both to enhance the practical decisions they make in case of later legal repercussions and to ascertain that their ethical/professional responses to the Code are *within the law*. The legal aspects of each clause of the Code are examined and the legal and professional arguments are compared and contrasted. Liberal use is made of practical examples covering a wide range of nursing situations, both in the hospital and the community, general and psychiatric nursing, children and the elderly and the special needs of students, the newly qualified, ward sisters and nurse managers are all considered. Relevant legal cases are also quoted. Where necessary, some details have been altered to respect confidentiality.

For clarity, the nurse throughout this book is designated 'she' as the majority of nurses are female and other professionals are designated 'he'. If not obvious from the text, patients are also designated 'he'.

As the UKCC Code of Professional Conduct is issued to all UK nurses, the law quoted can be assumed to apply in essentials throughout the United Kingdom unless otherwise stated. Any marked differences in Scottish or Northern Ireland law will be mentioned in the text as appropriate.

Preface to Second Edition

The two years since publication of the first edition have seen massive change to nurses working both within the National Health Service and elsewhere. As well as the far-reaching effects of the NHS and Community Care Act 1990, other important recent legislation has affected how the nurse carries out her professional responsibilities. In addition, a wealth of new case law has begun to address some of the most knotty of ethical problems relating to patients' rights.

Not surprisingly, the UKCC decided, after widespread consultation, to issue a new edition of the Code of Professional Conduct. Most of it is still familiar. However, apart from some rewording, there are now sixteen clauses instead of fourteen and the additional material is a particular reflection of the changing environment in which nurses practise.

This second edition knits together both the new legal material and the changes to the Code within the original format of the first edition. Up-to-date practical illustrations have been added in a number of areas.

January 1993

Acknowledgements

Thanks to HMSO, Lewisham and North Southwark Health Authority, the United Kingdom Central Council and Alfred Hinde Printers for permission to reproduce material.

My thanks go to the staff of Scutari Press for their continuing enthusiasm, to Alys McGruddy for her typing and to Robert for his encouragement and support.

Finally, this book is particularly in memory of three dear friends who are no longer with us.

Table of Cases

Table of Statutes

The Nursing Profession and the Law

A staff nurse on night duty expressed concern at the fact that another registered nurse was frequently borrowing pethidine from her ward and suggested that the stock on the other ward must be inadequate. This comment led to an investigation that showed that the nurse in question had been obtaining pethidine from many wards within what was a large hospital. Further, this 'borrowing' was occurring when the ward stock on the nurse's ward was adequate. It was also found that fictitious treatment cards were being used. The nurse concerned had, over a period of months, gone to other wards with treatment cards, saying, 'I have to give this patient some pethidine and I have run out. Can I borrow some?' The registered nurses in these wards were providing the ampoules of pethidine, recording the entry in the Controlled Drugs book and signing that the drug had been given to the patient without witnessing this, in spite of such action being contrary to hospital policy. In some instances the procedure was repeated with the same ward three times in the course of a single night and, over a period of time, the nurse illegally and fraudulently obtained a very large quantity of pethidine (Pyne 1992).

The nurse in the above example fell foul of the law in three ways. She was convicted of a crime, was dismissed from her job and her name was removed from the Register. In fact, the law impinges on the profession of nursing in these and a number of other ways (see Figure I.1).

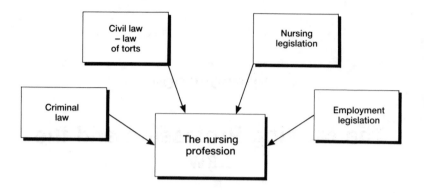

Figure I.1 The nursing profession and the law

Criminal law

A crime is an offence committed against the State either in the performance of some act which the law forbids or in the omission of some act which the law requires. For example, theft is a crime, as would be the wrongful use of controlled drugs under the Misuse of Drugs Act 1971 and its associated regulations. The outcome of a prosecution is guilty or not guilty (or, in addition, not proven in Scotland) and the penalties vary from fines to imprisonment.

There may be a legally recognised reason why an act, normally a legal wrong, is not so in certain circumstances. This is known as a defence. For example, in criminal law there may be a lack of capacity to form the necessary intention. A person suffering from a severe defect of reason may be found 'not guilty by reason of insanity'. The ability of a child to form the necessary intention will vary with age, the younger the child the more likely that he or she has no 'mischievous intention'. Self-defence may also be a defence, but any force used must only be that which is necessary to protect staff and others from harm and reasonably proportionate to the force being shown (Padfield 1983).

Civil law

This part of the law involves the rights and duties individuals have towards each other. Legal action is taken by a private individual against another individual or organisation. The outcome of a successful action is the award of monetary compensation to the wronged individual. Much of the professional's work is within the framework of civil law, particularly the part of it known as the law of torts (delicts in Scotland).

Negligence, hinging on the concept of duty of care, is a common notion in nursing as well as in law (Young 1989) and occurs where there is harm resulting from a failure in this duty. Trespass to the person is also known as assault and battery and a knowledge of this tort, along with how the legal defences of consent and urgency operate, is vital to the nurse. A third tort of interest to the nurse is defamation, either as libel or slander (in Scotland slander is treated more like assault and battery). These three torts are discussed in detail during the course of this book as they are of such major concern in professional practice.

Occasionally a civil wrong may also be a crime. Assault and battery and gross negligence both fall into this category.

Employment legislation

Much of the law relating to employment has its roots in civil law but, due to the increasing complexity of the work situation in recent years, the majority of this is now codified in Acts of Parliament. The two main themes running through this legislation are the protection of the individual employee and the regulation of industrial relations between employers and unions (Capper 1989). The Employment Protection (Consolidation) Act 1978 has been particularly important in clarifying the nature of the contractual position between employer and employee as well as laying down some of the ground-rules relating to trade union activity. Later Employment Acts have added to and extended the legal obligations of all parties. The nurse in the example on p. 1 would have been dismissed on the grounds of misconduct, a reason clearly defined and accepted in law.

Nursing legislation

There have been a number of Acts relating to nursing, the most recent being the Nurses, Midwives and Health Visitors Acts 1979 and 1992. Much of the law controlling nursing is enacted by a system of delegated legislation. The United Kingdom Central

Council is empowered by the Act to draw up such legislation; this is known as the Nurses Rules (e.g. Statutory Instruments 1983).

The UKCC's Legal and Professional Functions

The United Kingdom Central Council (UKCC) has 60 members, 40 of whom are elected by the profession. This significant change in the 1992 Act from previous legislation both enlarges the Council and makes it better able to perform a heavy workload satisfactorily. It has four main functions:

1. To establish and improve standards of training and professional conduct for nurses, midwives and health visitors.
2. To determine the rules for registration and maintain the single professional Register.
3. To provide guidance to the profession on standards of professional conduct.
4. To act, through the appropriate committees, to protect the public from unsafe members of the profession.

In addition to the Central Council, the Act set up four executive National Boards for England, Scotland, Wales and Northern Ireland. They consist of a smaller number of appointed members. Their main functions are:

1. To arrange courses enabling people to qualify for registration and courses of further training meeting the requirements of the Central Council as to their content and standard.
2. To arrange for examinations to be held.
3. To work with the Council to promote and improve training methods.

It is important to the profession that standards of nursing are maintained. The Council and the National Boards are directed to this professional aim by means of the law, the underlying motivation being the protection of the public rather than preservation of the professional interest.

The UKCC has the responsibility for determining when and how a person may be removed from the Register or otherwise disciplined. It does this by initially investigating allegations of misconduct and deciding whether referral to the Council's Professional Conduct Committee (in some situations the Health Committee) is necessary. If misconduct is proved the Committee has four options

– removal from the Register, suspension from the Register, administration of a formal caution or no action (UKCC 1992a).

Over the last few years, the number of nurses appearing before the professional conduct committee and the resulting number whose names were removed from the Register has increased (UKCC 1991). It is likely that this was owing to a heightening professional awareness of the importance of reporting cases of alleged misconduct in order to safeguard the patient. In the past, it may have been deemed sufficient to dismiss from employment but this would not necessarily prevent the nurse taking employment elsewhere. The commonest areas where misconduct is alleged are medical/surgical wards and in the area of mental illness and mental handicap. The commonest reasons for removal from the Register are for 'practice-related offences'. These include 'insensitivity or unkindness to patients' relatives, reckless or unskilful practice, obscene or indecent language in patient areas, concealing untoward incidents, misleading vulnerable patients, neglecting duties, failure to keep essential records, failure to summon emergency aid, falsifying records, failure to protect or promote patients' interests and failure to act when knowing that a colleague is improperly treating or abusing patients'. Theft, drug offences and other abuse of patients are also categories where a number of nurses are found guilty of professional misconduct. The relatively new category of 'abusing management power' shows an increase in numbers reported as well as in those removed from the Register.

The law defines misconduct as 'conduct unworthy of a nurse'. The measure against which a nurse's performance must be judged is the United Kingdom Central Council's Code of Professional Conduct (UKCC 1992b). Although the Code does not have the status of law, the UKCC issues it to all registered nurses, midwives and health visitors and 'requires members to practise and conduct themselves within the standards and framework provided by the Code', thus laying a professional duty on every individual. As the profession can legally prevent a nurse practising if she fails to measure up to the standards required, the law and professional behaviour remain intertwined.

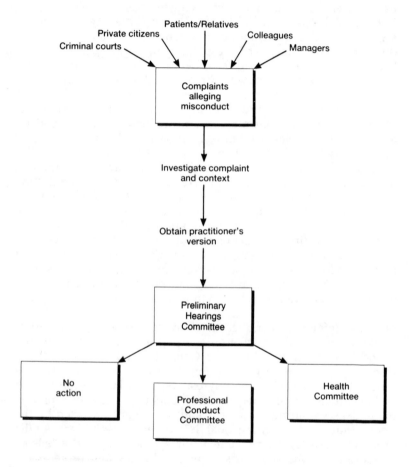

Figure I.2 The progress of complaints of misconduct through the nurses' statutory machinery

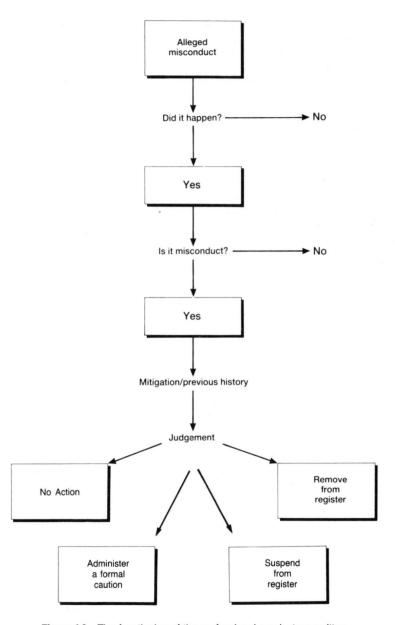

Figure I.3 The functioning of the professional conduct committee

References

Capper A 1989. Employment legislation. Checks and Balances. *Diploma in Nursing*. Distance Learning Centre, South Bank Polytechnic, London.

Padfield C 1983. *Law Made Simple*, revised by F. E. Smith, 6th edition. Heinemann, London.

Pyne R H 1992. *Professional Discipline in Nursing*, 2nd edition. Basil Blackwell, Oxford.

Statutory Instruments 1983. *Nurses, Midwives and Health Visitors Rules*. Approval Order No. 873. HMSO, London.

United Kingdom Central Council 1991. *Annual Report 1989–1990*. UKCC, London.

United Kingdom Central Council 1992a. Changes in Professional Conduct Affairs, *Register*, Autumn 1992, p. 5. UKCC, London.

United Kingdom Central Council 1992b. *The Code of Professional Conduct*, 3rd edition. UKCC, London.

Young A P 1989. *Legal Problems in Nursing Practice*, 2nd edition. Harper & Row, London.

CHAPTER 1

Patients' Interests

Act always in such a manner as to promote and safeguard the interests and well-being of patients and clients.

The first clause in the Code of Professional Conduct embraces such a wide spectrum of professional behaviour that it can be seen as a thread running throughout most of the remaining statements. The legal implications are similarly mirrored or extended later in the Code, but two main issues can be addressed in this chapter. First, the safeguarding of patients' well-being seems to be particularly concerned with the provision of safe care – a major concern of the law. Secondly, promoting and safeguarding patients' interests suggests not just the advocacy role of the nurse on the patient's behalf but the whole arena of the nurse's responsibilities in relation to patients' consent to treatment.

Safe care

Consider the following examples of nursing care.

1. A nurse puts a hot drink on the table in front of a hemiplegic patient. As the patient attempts to lift the cup to his mouth, he spills the hot fluid and scalds himself.
2. A patient complains of severe pain after an operation and this pain continues for several days longer than would normally be expected. The nurses concerned give analgesia to control the pain but fail to record or report to the doctor the abnormal pattern displayed. As a result, serious complications ensue which might have been minimised if early action had been taken.

3. A nurse gives faulty advice to a patient concerning his diet and lifestyle after a myocardial infarction.

In each of these cases, the professional view is likely to be that the patient's well-being has not been safeguarded, most immediately in the first example, but even in the third example harm could result to the patient over a period of time. The law would support the professional concern to some extent, mainly through the law relating to negligence. However, responsibility and causation have to be clearly shown. The scalded patient would therefore be likely to have a strong case against the nurse, and even the patient in the second example might be able to show some contributory negligence on the part of the nurses subsequent to that of the surgeon. However, if the third patient had a further myocardial infarction it would be impossible to put the blame on the nurse giving faulty advice as so many other factors could have affected the patient's health. Therefore the legal view would, in this instance, be unable to support the professional view.

Merely by using such simple examples, it can be shown that the law's concern with the well-being of the patient is going to be of a different nature from that of the professional, perhaps even of a different level. The professional standard should be set at giving excellent care although it has to be stated that the day-to-day realities may make this goal difficult to attain. But whatever the constraints, the minimal professional standard must be to give safe care. The law supports the notion of safety rather than excellence in a number of ways. In *Bolam* v. *Friern HMC* 1957, the judge stated that the medical standard of care was the standard of a reasonably skilled and experienced doctor (see p. 29) and the *Wilsher* case highlighted the importance of the patient being guaranteed safe care in spite of inexperienced medical staff. It seems likely that the same criteria apply to nursing staff. (For a full discussion of the law relating to negligence, see Chapter 2.)

Harm inflicted on patients

Florence Nightingale's statement that 'the hospital should do the patient no harm' (Nightingale 1859) cannot in reality be maintained. Some harm is avoidable, as illustrated in the three examples above, and this type of damage is that which is potentially under the legal negligence umbrella. But there are many occasions when a patient chooses to risk harming himself when agreeing to surgery or medication. The former will cause some mutilation, even if this is temporary; the latter may have unpleasant side-effects. The law dealing with consent is therefore vital when considering the interests of patients or clients and the rest of this chapter will look at the nurse's responsibilities and the patient's rights in this area.

A legally valid consent

Consent can be obtained in a number of different ways. Sometimes consent can be assumed. The Medical Defence Union (1986) states that for most physical contact between doctor and patient consent is implied by the voluntary actions of the patient. Legally the nurse's situation is similar. For example, a patient coming into hospital on a voluntary basis or allowing the community nurse into his home is implying consent to the care offered. The patient's action in holding out his hand for his tablets is an example of this. From a professional point of view, the nurse may feel that it is in the patient's interest always to gain express consent rather than make any assumptions, but in practice assuming consent works well as long as the nurse only relies on this when no harm is likely to result from the care given and the patient is not expressing any reservations.

Express consent 'can be oral or written and should be obtained for any procedure which carries a special risk' (Medical Defence Union 1986). Both doctors and nurses use oral consent. A doctor taking a blood sample asks the patient for his consent (he should also gain consent for the tests to be carried out on the blood sample although this is not always done). A nurse seeks the patient's oral consent before washing him. In fact, this oral route is the one most used by nurses.

Where investigations or treatments carry a marked risk, the patient's written consent is advised and this will always be the doctor's responsibility. The law does not specifically state when consent should be written rather than oral, but traditionally any surgery, general anaesthetic or investigation carrying a risk of death or severe damage will use a written format. However, some variations will be observed between different health authorities or even between doctors working for the same employer. The nurse can feel satisfied that the patient's interests have been safeguarded as long as a valid consent has been obtained whether orally or in writing. However, she may want to query the use of an oral consent if the usual practice in that area is for a written consent, but must accept that it is the doctor's right to decide the nature of the consent gained.

A person can give a legally valid consent if he has the 'capacity to understand and come to a decision on what is involved and the capacity to communicate that decision' (Skegg 1984). Even a child under sixteen years can give consent in an emergency if he has that understanding, although it is usual to ask a patient or guardian if at all possible. A woman gives consent for any treatment in the same way as a man (Faulder 1985), even when treatment results in abortion, and there is no legal requirement for her partner's consent. Nurses may also be involved in discussing possible care or treatments with patients' relatives in other situations. However, although it is important in some instances to gain the relatives' cooperation, the law is quite clear that no relative has the authority to give consent for another adult. (For further discussion of what action can be taken if a patient is unable to give consent, see p. 18.)

The nurse can play an important part in assisting the patient in giving an effective consent. First, she will be in a strong position to assess whether the patient has the necessary capacity to understand owing to the 24-hour contact the nurse has with the patient, compared to the minutes that the doctor can give to just one of many patients under his care. Secondly, if the patient has difficulty in communicating his intentions and wishes, the nurse can act as an interpreter. For example, a patient with severe Parkinson's disease may have very slow and distorted speech, but over a period of time the nurse can come to understand what that patient is saying. However, she must always remember that her role is to assist the patient to reach his own decisions and never to persuade the patient to her views (see Chapter 5).

The timing of the consent in relation to the care or treatment to be carried out is of interest. Nurses may be very concerned that the doctor interviewing the patient on admission to hospital for surgery gives very minimal information before requiring the patient to sign a consent form. However, information may be given to a patient over a period of time, starting in the outpatient department when the patient is probably seen by the consultant or senior registrar, not a house officer. In this way, it is likely that the patient's interests have been safeguarded. Similarly, if for any reason a treatment is postponed or repeated, the original consent can still be regarded as valid unless circumstances have changed in the meantime. At the other extreme, all nurses should be aware that patients who have been given sedation or premedication prior to an investigation or surgery are in no fit state to give a valid consent, so if for some reason the gaining of consent has been overlooked until after such drugs have been given, the treatment will have to be delayed.

Informed consent

The concept of informed consent probably originated early this century but was particularly applied to medical experimentation during the Nuremberg Trials in 1947. It is usually considered to be the process whereby explicit communication of information is provided and included in this are not only details of the treatment to be carried out but also of the risks involved.

However, a number of legal cases in the United Kingdom have made it clear that the patient's right to full information is limited (Brazier 1987).

Miss Chatterton complained of severe pain in a post-operative scar. After two operations to relieve this pain, she was no better and in addition to the pain, she now had loss of sensation in her right leg and foot, with some loss of mobility. She sued Dr Gerson, claiming that he had failed to give her sufficient information for an informed consent. She lost her case (*Chatterton* v. *Gerson* 1981), the judge stating that the consent was valid provided that the patient was 'informed in broad terms of the nature of the procedure which is intended'.

The Sidaway case raised several additional issues (*Sidaway* v. *Board of Governors of the Bethlem Royal and Maudsley Hospital* 1984 and 1985).

Mrs Sidaway had persistent pain in the right arm and shoulder following an accident at work, the pain later spreading to the left arm. In 1974 the doctor diagnosed pressure on the nerve root as the cause of pain. An operation was carried out to relieve this pressure but the result was that Mrs Sidaway became partially paralysed. She complained that Mr Falconer, the surgeon, had failed to warn her of the risk of injury to the spinal cord (this risk was less than 1 per cent).

Mrs Sidaway's claim failed both at the original hearing and at appeal, for the following reasons:

1. The doctor would have warned the patient in general terms of possible injury to the nerve root and the patient understood the general nature of the proposed surgery.
2. The doctor has a duty to warn patients of risks, but providing he conformed to a responsible body of medical opinion in deciding what to tell or not to tell, that duty was discharged properly.
3. Only if a consent is obtained by fraud or misrepresentation is that consent not a true consent.
4. The patient had not expressly asked about the risks and the doctor could not be faulted for failing to give information not asked for.
5. A doctor can withhold information if it can be shown that a reasonable medical assessment of the patient would indicate that disclosure of information would pose a 'serious threat of psychological detriment to the patient'.

Sometimes a patient may be more likely to win a legal battle by suing for negligence rather than battery. However, Mrs Sidaway failed in this as well, as did Mr Bolam (*Bolam* v. *Friern Hospital Management Committee* 1957). This case of negligence included suing for failure of the consultant to disclose the risk of fracture as a result of electroconvulsive therapy without anaesthetic (the accepted practice at that time). The judge found in favour of the doctor as he had practised his professional skills according to accepted medical standards. In addition, the doctor cannot be criticised for not stressing those dangers which he believes to be minimal.

To the nurse whose concern for safeguarding her patient's interests must take precedence over supporting the legal perspective of her medical colleagues, the above must make for depressing reading. However, there are many doctors who pursue the idea of informed consent to a marked degree regardless of the law's view that this is unnecessary. In addition there is a number of ways in which the nurse can promote the sharing of information from doctor to patient.

The nurse's role

A patient's ability to understand and therefore reach an informed decision may be restricted by his intelligence, education, or grasp of English. While some doctors make a particular effort to explain to and educate their patients regarding their condition and treatments, this is not always the case. The elderly are particularly vulnerable (Age Concern 1986). Problems of hearing and an awe of doctors may limit the ability of an old person to take in information and sadly some people tend to treat the old as if they were children. Medical terminology may thwart understanding and the nurse can play an important part in reinforcing the doctor's information. She can explain in words the patient can understand and repeat information that the patient has been too anxious to take in the first time.

Patients will vary in the extent to which they wish to be informed. As demonstrated in the Sidaway case, the patient needs to ask if detailed information is required. The nurse can assist by phrasing the patient's questions to the doctor, or by giving the patient additional information if she feels satisfied that she can clarify some of the patient's queries. However, the nurse must remember that she could be sued if the patient suffered harm as a result of her giving wrong information. If the patient wants more information than the nurse is competent to give, then her duty is to refer these queries back to the doctor. The nurse should also respect the wishes of the patient who does not want detailed information.

As mentioned above, the doctor may restrict the amount of knowledge given to a patient if he considers that detailed information could be detrimental to the patient's condition. Potentially, the nurse can be of assistance in assessing the patient's state of mind.

The nature of the treatment will also affect the amount of information given to a patient. Generally, the less essential a procedure is to the health of the patient, the greater the obligation to give detailed information. In *Blyth* v. *Bloomsbury AHA* 1985, damages were awarded when a sterilisation operation failed and a child was born, as the woman was not warned of the risk. The difference to the Sidaway case was that the sterilisation was carried out for convenience, not medical necessity. The nurse should bear this in mind when assisting her patients to gain the proper amount of information. By contrast, a very ill patient requiring urgent surgery in order to save his life may be given minimal information and still give a valid consent and it would be quite inappropriate for the nurse to tire the patient with further explanation unless he specifically wanted this.

Treatment that is of variable use to the patient is experimental work carried out as part of research. Using the above guidelines regarding the amount of information and the degree of medical necessity, it is advisable to give considerable detail of risks involved. Two codes spell out this requirement, the Nuremberg Code and the Declaration of Helsinki (Dyer 1992). The latter states:

> In any research on human beings each potential subject must be adequately informed of the aims, methods, anticipated benefits and potential hazards of the study and the discomfort it may entail. He should be informed that he is at liberty to abstain from participation at any time.

Following these rules would certainly safeguard the patient's interests but unfortunately the Code has no legal status. It may be particularly hard for nurses to remain objective when instigating a patient's treatment regime, knowing that there are others as potentially beneficial. It may be that as the patient is part of a research programme, no choice is given. The nurse may also have been told not to give the patient any specific facts about the experimental treatment which, while in the interests of the research and the future benefit of patients, is difficult to equate with the immediate situation.

The nurse also has a role to play if the patient changes his mind. Even if the patient has signed a consent form, that consent can be withdrawn at any time. As it is usually the nurse who is with the patient at this time, her responsibility is clearly to inform the doctor and delay the treatment, even if the patient has been pre-medicated and is on his way to the operating theatre! Similarly, if a patient expresses grave doubts regarding the proposed treatment after having given consent, the doctor must be informed and a written note made in the nursing records of what has transpired.

Finally, it is sometimes difficult for nurses to accept a patient's refusal to give consent, particularly when the treatment being offered is life-saving (see p. 87). For example, a patient with cancer of the bowel has been offered a partial colectomy. An 80-year-old patient refusing such an operation may arouse different emotions in the nurse compared to a 40-year-old patient doing the same thing. However, the nurse must always remember that the patient has the right to choose and her role is to support the patient in this right. There is a temptation to overrule a patient's refusal on the assumption that he is not really capable of making a decision. Culver and Gert (1982) gave a useful ruling on this stating, 'a patient's apparently irrational refusal of consent should never be taken as a sign of incompetence if, were it to have been given in

CONSENT FORM

For medical or dental investigation, treatment or operation

Health Authority	Patient's Surname ....
Hospital	Other Names ....
Unit Number.................................	Date of Birth ....
	Sex: *(please tick)* Male ☐ Female ☐

DOCTORS OR DENTISTS *(This part to be completed by doctor or dentist. See notes on the reverse)*

TYPE OF OPERATION INVESTIGATION OR TREATMENT

I confirm that I have explained the operation investigation or treatment, and such appropriate options as are available and the type of anaesthetic, if any (general/regional/sedation) proposed, to the patient in terms which in my judgement are suited to the understanding of the patient and/or to one of the parents or guardians of the patient

Signature.................................... Date ... / ... / .....

Name of doctor or dentist ....

PATIENT/PARENT/GUARDIAN

1. Please read this form and the notes overleaf very carefully.

2. If there is anything that you don't understand about the explanation, or if you want more information, you should ask the doctor or dentist.

3. Please check that all the information on the form is correct. If it is, and you understand the explanation, then sign the form.

I am the patient/parent/guardian *(delete as necessary)*

I agree	■ to what is proposed which has been explained to me by the doctor/dentist named on this form.
	■ to the use of the type of anaesthetic that I have been told about.
I understand	■ that the procedure may not be done by the doctor/dentist who has been treating me so far.
	■ that any procedure in addition to the investigation or treatment described on this form will only be carried out if it is necessary and in my best interests and can be justified for medical reasons.
I have told	■ the doctor or dentist about any additional procedures I would not wish to be carried out straightaway without my having the opportunity to consider them first.

Signature	....
Name	....
Address	....
(if not the patient)	....
	....

NHS *Management Executive*

Figure 1.1 Sample consent form   (continued overleaf)

NOTES TO:

Doctors, Dentists

A patient has a legal right to grant or withhold consent prior to examination or treatment. Patients should be given sufficient information, in a way they can understand, about the proposed treatment and the possible alternatives. Patients must be allowed to decide whether they will agree to the treatment and they may refuse or withdraw consent to treatment at any time. The patient's consent to treatment should be recorded on this form (further guidance is given in HC(90)22 *(A Guide to Consent for Examination or Treatment.)*

Patients

■ The doctor or dentist is here to help you. He or she will explain the proposed treatment and what the alternatives are. You can ask any questions and seek further information. You can refuse the treatment.

■ You may ask for a relative, or friend, or a nurse to be present.

■ Training health professionals is essential to the continuation of the health service and improving the quality of care. Your treatment may provide an important opportunity for such training, where necessary under the careful supervision of a senior doctor or dentist. You may refuse any involvement in a formal training programme without this adversely affecting your care and treatment.

the same circumstances, the consent would have been regarded as valid'.

Inability to give consent

So far, the position of the nurse promoting the patients' interests has concentrated on those patients who are able to give a legally valid consent. What part can and should the nurse play with those who are unable to give their consent?

Patients who lack the necessary capacity to give a valid consent are the unconscious, some of the mentally ill and the mentally confused. In most cases it is in the patient's interests to give treatment or care that will save the person's life. The law is seemingly very clear on this point, using the criteria of urgency and necessity and therefore allowing doctors to carry out 'essential procedures which are necessary to save life or prevent serious damage to health' (National Consumer Council 1983).

For the unconscious it is therefore legal for treatment to be carried out without consent, using the criteria of both urgency and necessity, but not any inessential treatment. This view is also valid when a patient is unconscious under anaesthesia. In *Beatty* v. *Illingworth* 1896, both ovaries were removed in spite of the woman's specific wish that she should not be deprived of the ability to have children, the legal view being that both ovaries were so diseased that if the patient had known this, she would have agreed. The element of urgency must exist in all these cases (see wording on sample consent form, Figure 1.1, p. 17). The nurse may sometimes meet situations where she may query the necessity of treatment on the grounds that the patient cannot be saved and treatment is then being performed unnecessarily to the detriment of the patient's dignity (see p. 88).

The mentally ill have the same rights regarding consent as anyone else, except in a few instances (Dyer and Bloch 1987). The Mental Health Act 1983 has strict criteria regarding consent and on the whole the patient's interests are safeguarded. It is impossible to perform psychosurgery without consent, and even electroconvulsive therapy is only possible without consent after consultation with a number of professionals including the nurse (see p. 80). In certain circumstances, urgent treatment can be given. The *Code of Practice* 1990 suggests the following criteria for proceeding without consent:

> when the patient is incapable of giving consent by reason of the fact that he is suffering from a mental disorder which is leading to behaviour that is an immediate serious danger to himself or to other people and it is not possible immediately to apply the provisions of the Mental Health Act (where treatment is a proper response in order to achieve the minimum necessary to avert that danger).

The situation is a little different in Northern Ireland where the Mental Health Act 1961 has not yet been revised in line with the rest of the United Kingdom. On the whole, the issue of consent can be dealt with on the same lines as described above, except that the Northern Ireland Act does not spell out the procedures to be followed when psychotherapy and electroconvulsive therapy are prescribed.

Mental confusion can be an ongoing component of both mental and physical illness. The capacity of the patient to give a valid consent is markedly reduced. The underlying principle of urgency and necessity can be used to some extent, but is limited in two ways. First, the confusion may be long term and the legal basis of proceeding without consent is based only on the short-term situ-

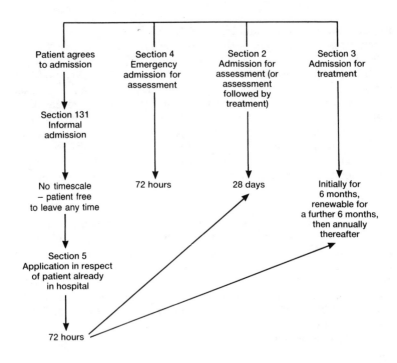

Figure 1.2 Civil admission of the mentally disordered patient to hospital

ation. Secondly, not to proceed with care or treatment until the situation becomes urgent is rarely good professional practice as the patient's prognosis may be impoverished as a result. The Mental Health Act 1983 could be used and the patient placed under section, thus allowing urgent treatment for the disorder causing the mental confusion for a period of three months, but this is an emotive step to take and is often distressing to relatives.

Several court cases have pointed the way for a different approach. In *T.* v. *T.* 1988 the courts supported the recommendation of the doctors that a severely mentally handicapped woman have an abortion and be sterilised. In *F.* v. *West Berkshire Health Authority* 1989, involving another mentally handicapped woman, the judge declared that as the woman was unable to give consent because of her lack of capacity, a sterilisation operation could go ahead as it was in F's 'best interests'. There is, therefore, in English law the notion of best interests of the patient where there is a long-term lack of capacity.

The NHS Management Executive (1990) gives some advice as to how such decisions should be made.

'In practice, a decision may involve others besides the doctor. It must surely be good practice to consult relatives and others who are concerned with the care of the patient. Sometimes, of course, consultation with a specialist or specialists will be required, and in others, especially where the decision involves more than a purely medical decision, an inter-disciplinary team will in practice participate in the decision.'

Such practice accords well with Clause 1 of the Code of Professional Conduct. However, as this document is only a guide, it does not give the nurse any legal authority of involvement.

Detention and restraint of patients

If, for the above reasons, the decision is made to treat a patient without his consent, or even against his active refusal to participate, the issue becomes one of when it is in the patient's interests to be detained or restrained against his will.

The mentally ill can be detained by law under various sections of the Mental Health Act 1983 for assessment or treatment (see Figure 1.2). The safeguards for the patient are quite strict and the patient must be told his rights both verbally and in writing (see Figure 1.3). The nurse may well be involved in ensuring that the patient understands his rights but will only occasionally be involved in the original detention order (see p. 77).

Under the Public Health Act 1936, the Public Health (Control of Diseases) Act 1984 and its associated Regulations 1985, patients suffering from certain diseases that are deemed to be a danger to others can be detained, with an order made by a magistrate or sheriff. Although not invoked often, these legal powers have been used with people suffering from certain infectious diseases, which could include AIDS. In these situations, the patient will be unwilling to be detained, hence the necessity of the order, but the nurse concerned has to think of interests wider than those of the patient.

A patient may be detained in hospital by the police if he has been arrested. The detention is scarcely in the patient's interests, but again is in the interests of society. Fortunately, the nurse is not involved in this detention although she may have to work around the police as she cares for the patient so detained!

Mental Health Act 1983 Leaflet 6
Section 2

Name _____

Your hospital doctor is _____

Date of admission _____

Your rights under the Mental Health Act 1983

Why you are being held

You are being held in this hospital/mental nursing home on the advice of two doctors. You can be kept here for up to 28 days (4 weeks) so that doctors can find out what is wrong and how they can help. You may also be given any treatment you may need while you are kept here. You must not leave before the end of the 28 days unless a doctor tells you that you can. If you try to leave before then the staff can stop you, and if you do leave you can be brought back. You can be held in this way because of Section 2 of the Mental Health Act 1983. These notes are to tell you what that means.

After 28 days you can only be kept in hospital if your doctor thinks you need to stay longer and makes new arrangements (under Section 3 of the Mental Health Act). If your doctor is thinking of doing this he will talk to you about it towards the end of the 28 days, and you will be given a further leaflet to explain your rights.

If you want to leave

The doctor will tell you when he thinks you are well enough to leave hospital. If you want to go before the end of the 28 days and before he says you are ready, you will have to get the agreement of either

- the hospital managers; or
- the Mental Health Review Tribunal

If you think you should be allowed to leave hospital you should talk to your doctor. If he thinks you should stay, but you still want to leave, you can ask the hospital

1

Figure 1.3 Your rights under the Mental Health Act 1983, page 1

managers to let you go. You should write to them to ask them to do this. Their address is

_____

_____

The Tribunal

You can also ask the Mental Health Review Tribunal to decide if you can leave hospital. You can ask the Tribunal to look at your case by writing to them or sending them a form which the hospital can give you. The Tribunal's address is

_____

_____

_____

You must write to the Tribunal in the first 14 days (2 weeks) of your stay in hospital. If you need help writing the letter or filling in the form your social worker or the hospital staff will help you.

There are usually three people on the Tribunal – a lawyer, a psychiatrist (doctor) and a third person who is not a doctor. All these people will come from outside the hospital.

If you ask the Tribunal to look at your case they will probably ask to see you and your doctor. If the Tribunal see you, they will be able to make sure that they have full details of your case, and you will be able to tell them yourself why you want to leave hospital. You may not have to see the Tribunal if you do not want to but you can insist on seeing them if you want. The doctor from the Tribunal will want to talk to you in any case. The Tribunal will listen to what you and your doctor say, and to what everyone else says, and then decide if you can leave hospital.

You can also ask someone, including a solicitor if you wish, to help you to ask the Tribunal to look at your case and help you put your views to the Tribunal. Because of the legal advice and assistance scheme this solicitor's help may be free or it may only cost you a little. The Tribunal office or social worker will tell you how to find a solicitor or other help if you ask them.

Your treatment

You are being kept in hospital to make sure that you get the medical treatment you need. Your doctor will talk to you about any treatment he thinks you need. In most cases you will have to accept his advice except in the case of certain treatments.

– If your doctor wants you to have certain very specialised and rare treatments he *must* have your agreement and he must get another doctor's opinion on

2

Figure 1.3 Your rights under the Mental Health Act 1983, page 2

the treatment that he wants you to have. You can withdraw your agreement at any time. The other doctor will have to talk to other staff who are involved in your case, including a nurse. The law protects you in other ways too. If your doctor wants you to have one of these treatments he will explain all this to you.

– If your doctor feels that you need to have ECT (electro convulsive therapy, sometimes called electric or shock treatment) and you agree, he can go ahead with the treatment. But if you do not agree, unless it is an emergency, he must first ask a doctor from outside the hospital to see you. This other doctor will talk to you and to other staff who are involved in your case, including a nurse, about the treatment and decide whether you need it. If the second doctor says you should have this treatment you will be given it.

– If at first you agree that your doctor may give you ECT but later you change your mind you should tell your doctor that you no longer agree to this treatment. He will then have to ask a doctor from outside the hospital to see you to decide whether you need to go on having it. Again, he will talk to other staff.

If you have any questions or complaints

If you want to ask something, or to complain about something, talk to the doctor, nurse or social worker. If you are not happy with the answer you may write to the hospital managers. If you are still not happy with the reply you are given you can ask the Mental Health Act Commission to help you. You can also write to the Commission even after you have left hospital.

The Mental Health Act Commission

The Commission was set up specially to make sure that the mental health law is used properly and that patients are cared for properly while they are kept in hospital. You can ask them to help you by writing to them at

_____

_____

_____

Your letters

Any letters sent to you will be given to you. You can send letters to anyone except a person who has said that he does not want to get letters from you. Letters to these people will be stopped by the hospital.

3

Figure 1.3 Your rights under the Mental Health Act 1983, page 3

Your nearest relative

A copy of these notes will be sent to your nearest relative who we have been told is

_____

If you do not want this to happen please tell the nurse in charge of your ward or a doctor. Your nearest relative can write to the hospital managers to ask them to let you leave. The managers will need at least 72 hours (3 full days) to consider such a request. so that your doctor can consider whether you should leave or not.

If there is anything in this leaflet you do not understand, the doctor or a nurse or social worker will help you. If you need help in writing a letter you should ask one of them, or a relative or friend.

Printed in UK for HMSO 8162037/29M/4.89/52523

4

Figure 1.3 Your rights under the Mental Health Act 1983, page 4
Reproduced with permission of HMSO

In both the detention of patients against their will or the giving of treatments without consent, the nurse may need to restrain the patient. The Royal College of Nursing has issued guidelines for nurses on this matter (1979), the essential legal points being the documentation of any instances of restraint and informing the doctor in charge and senior nursing personnel. (For further aspects of restraint, see Chapter 10.)

Conclusion

The law on negligence goes some way towards ensuring that the well-being of patients is safeguarded, but it is in the area of consent that the law seems less concerned with patients' interests than nurses, in their role as professional carers, would like. The law seems to support the right of the medical profession to know what is best for their patients, even when invoking recent case law in the area of the mentally handicapped. Legally, the courts have always supported the medical profession in their right to make such decisions. Nurses are left to promote and safeguard patients' interests largely on a professional, rather than a legal, basis.

References

Age Concern 1986. *The Law and Vulnerable Elderly People*. Age Concern, Mitcham, Surrey.
Brazier M 1987. *Medicine, Patients and the Law*. Penguin Books, Harmondsworth, Middlesex.
Culver C M and Gert B 1982 *Philosophy in Medicine*. Oxford University Press, Oxford.
Department of Health and Welsh Office. *1990 Code of Practice: Mental Health Act 1983*, HMSO, London.
Dyer C 1992 *Doctors, Patients and the Law*. Blackwell, Oxford.
Dyer A R and Bloch S 1987. Informed consent and the psychiatric patient. *Journal of Medical Ethics* **13**, pp. 12–16.
Faulder C 1985. *Whose Body Is It?* Virago, London.
Medical Defence Union 1986. *Consent to Treatment*. Medical Defence Union, London.
National Consumer Council 1983. *Patients' Right: A Guide for N.H.S. Patients and Doctors*. HMSO, London.
NHS Management Executive 1990. *A Guide to Consent for Examination on Treatment*, NHSME, Department of Health, London.
Nightingale F 1859. *Notes on Nursing* (reprinted 1970). Dent, London.
Royal College of Nursing 1979. *Seclusion and Restraint in Hospitals and Units for the Mentally Disordered*. RCN, London.
Skegg P D G 1984. *Law, Ethics and Medicine*. Clarendon Press, Oxford.
United Kingdom Central Council 1992. *Code of Professional Conduct*, 3rd edition. UKCC, London.

CHAPTER 2

Negligence

Ensure that no action or omission on your part, or within your sphere of responsibility, is detrimental to the interests, condition or safety of patients and clients.

Miss Campbell, a 75-year-old, had been in a geriatric ward for two months. She was severely disabled with advanced acromegaly, diabetes and failing eyesight. As a young woman she had been beautiful and a dancer by profession. In old age she was bitter and angry, both with fate and her fellow human beings. One evening she was given the wrong medication in error, receiving diazepam 5 mg, which should have been given to the patient in the next bed. Was the nurse concerned negligent?

Clause 2 of the Code of Professional Conduct is particularly concerned with negligence and bears a remarkable similarity to this particular legal tort. The definition of negligence was laid down in *Blyth* v. *Birmingham Water Works* 1891:

> Negligence is the omission to do something which a reasonable man, guided upon these considerations which ordinarily regulate the conduct of human affairs, would do, or to do something which a prudent and reasonable man would not do.

Three main points must be included:

1. The plaintiff must prove that the defendant owed him a legal duty of care.
2. He must prove that there has been a breach of that duty.

3. He must prove consequential damage which must not be too remote from the cause of the accident (Padfield 1983).

(In Scotland, the defendant is known as the defender and the plaintiff the pursuer.)

In law a person must take reasonable care to avoid acts or omissions which he can reasonably foresee as being likely to injure his neighbour, defined as 'a person who is so closely and directly affected by one's act that one ought reasonably to have them in contemplation as being so affected when one is directing one's mind to the acts or omissions being called in question' (Lord Atkin in *Donoghue* v. *Stevenson* 1932).

Clause 2 of the Code mentions both acts and omissions; 'detrimental to the interests, or safety of patients' seems to have links with 'consequential damage'. However, it should be pointed out that there is one important difference between the professional and legal viewpoints. What happened to Miss Campbell in the example above is likely to be professional negligence. To give the wrong drug to a patient may not necessarily be detrimental to her condition, but must cause concern as to her safety as it reflects on the competence of the nurse and the effectiveness of the regulations concerning drug administration. However, for negligence in law, the third point of consequential damage could not be proved in Miss Campbell's case. In fact, the morning following the drug error, the nurse involved was greeted by a smiling Miss Campbell who stated that she had had the best night's sleep of her whole stay in hospital!

The three aspects required for legal proof of negligence will now be looked at in more detail.

Duty of care

It would seem obvious that nurses owe a duty of care to their patients. Staff talk of being on duty and their contractual position underlines the giving of care as part of their work.

However, the application of this duty is not as clear as it seems. The law does not accept that when a nurse is off duty, she no longer has a duty of care. As was seen in the definition of neighbour, everyone has a duty of care towards others, although it may be fairly minimal. For the nurse, the duty of care she displays is expected to be of a higher degree *at all times*. Thus if she goes to assist when someone in the street is involved in an accident, she could be sued for negligence if harm resulted from a failure of the nurse to give the standard of care expected of a nurse. The legal answer to this predicament is to avoid giving assistance in these situations or admitting to being a nurse. The former is scarcely professional behaviour and the latter may be impossible for the community nurse who has to travel in uniform between patients. Even when on duty, the nurse's duty of care has to be wider than that owed to her patients. Relatives and visitors are also owed a duty, although to a lesser extent, and certainly she must bear in mind the effect of acts or omissions on her colleagues. (This last point is discussed in depth in Chapter 9.)

The interface between hospital and the public is often the casualty department. Here the law states that a person presenting himself in the Accident and Emergency Department can expect to be treated. In *Barnett* v. *Chelsea and Kensington HMC* 1969, the doctor was criticised for not coming to the Casualty Department to examine the patient. There is a clear duty of care to treat those who present themselves. Interestingly, in the above case, the negligence claim failed on the grounds that even if the doctor had attended, the patient would still have died; causation could not be proved. For the nursing staff, sending a patient away untreated could potentially be negligence.

The nature of the duty of care needs further discussion. As already pointed out, the concept of reasonable behaviour is important in law, and for the professional this becomes a major concern. In *Bolam* v. *Friern HMC* 1957 (see p. 14), the judge explored this issue: 'the medical standard of care is the standard of a reasonably skilled and experienced doctor.' And, 'It is well-established law that it is sufficient if he exercises the ordinary skill of an ordinary competent man exercising that particular art.'

Two later cases have further clarified these concepts: 'A doctor who professes to exercise a special skill must exercise the ordinary skill of his speciality' (*Maynard* v. *W. Midlands RHA* 1984) and in *Whitehouse* v. *Jordan* 1981, the House of Lords stated that clinical judgement is included in the standard expected of an ordinary skilled doctor.

Although all these cases referred to doctors and medical practice, the rulings are applicable to nurses and nursing practice wherever carried out. A full exploration as to what constitutes an ordinary nurse takes place in Chapter 3, but it must be clear from the above that the law does not expect nurses to be superhuman.

Acts or omissions

The possibility of negligent acts or omissions is endless. Some of the more common will be explored.

The theatre nurse is particularly vulnerable when there are long lists, staff shortages and critically ill patients. This is also one area where suing for negligence is most likely to be successful, either because of wrong operations or swabs or instruments being left inside patients. In *Urry and Urry* v. *Bierer* 1955, the fact that a pack was left inside the patient was proof of negligence without any further need to explore individual responsibility; several later cases have upheld this principle. These negligent acts are of such concern to both the medical and nursing professions that joint guidelines have been issued by the Medical Defence Union and the Royal College of Nursing (1978). Giving wrong drugs, as in the example at the start of this chapter, is unfortunately also common and wrong dosages of drugs equally so. In this latter example, the negligence may well be shared between doctor and nurse if the prescription is wrong, but the nurse fails to notice this. If the drug is a reasonably common one in that area, the nurse should have the knowledge to know the normal dose and therefore question the prescription and, if no acceptable explanation is forthcoming, to refuse to give the drug (see p. 101). Some further examples of negligent acts are given in Chapter 1 (p. 9).

Failure to give proper care may be negligence. Omitting to give a prescribed drug without adequate reason, not turning a paralysed patient two-hourly, not observing the safety of a secluded patient at fifteen-minute intervals are all potentially negligent if harm resulted. In fact, similar examples have led to successful legal actions, not necessarily because the nurses concerned did omit the proper care, but because they failed to report or document their actions. A court will tend to find in the plaintiff's favour if there is a lack of evidence. (Proper documentation in negligence is so important that it is dealt with as a separate issue on p. 33.)

Negligent acts or omissions leading to the death of the patient may be classified as gross negligence and lead to a criminal charge of murder or manslaughter. For murder, there must usually be the necessary intention and it is extremely unlikely that a negligent omission of care could lead to this charge (see Dr Arthur's case, p. 75).

Industrial action may lead to negligence if patients are harmed as a result, for example by a nurse going on strike. The professional view was originally stated by the General Nursing Council in 1979.

> The Council is of the opinion that if a nurse puts the health, safety and welfare of her patients at risk by taking strike or other industrial action, she would have a case to answer on the score of professional misconduct, just as she would if the health, safety or welfare of patients were put at risk by any other action on her part.

More recently, the United Kingdom Central Council has pointed out to nurses contemplating industrial action that they could face disciplinary action by the professional conduct committee on the basis of clauses 1 and 2 of the Code, although it would be 'wrong to assume that every piece of industrial action will necessarily put patients at risk' (UKCC 1989).

To take industrial action is, of course, quite legal for nurses, although, for strike action, a properly run, secret ballot of the members of the union or professional body must take place. To assist in the interpretation of the relevant employment legislation, codes of practice have been drawn up and in this area they state that those employees having special obligations arising from membership of a profession should not be called upon by their union to take action conflicting with professional conduct. However, these codes are not legally binding.

Consequential damage

Resultant damage can be physical or psychological, and the courts will award damages for each. If there is contributory negligence on the part of the plaintiff, the amount of compensation awarded will be reduced.

Although the aim of a legal case is to award financial recompense to the damaged plaintiff, the professional feels very much as if the aim is to apportion blame. The nature of the court supports a combative scenario which destroys any positive relationship between professional and patient.

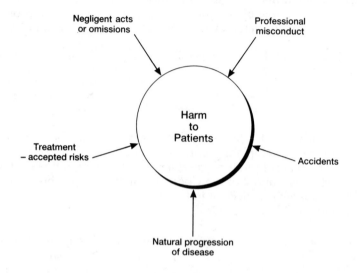

Figure 2.1 Sources of harm to patients

Although it is important that the professional does take blame when this is appropriate, the mechanism could follow the professional conduct route as long as this is seen to be done properly and carry sufficient weight to prevent similar errors occurring in the future. The *Code of Professional Conduct* (1992) is already used by the UKCC's professional conduct committee to discipline nurses, with the possible removal of the nurse's name from the Register (see p. 4). However, there have been criticisms of the committee's standards where misconduct has had to be proved. As a result, its practices are now regularly reviewed and the level of proof required is as high as in any court of law.

Another problem is that many patients suffer harm that cannot be proved to be negligence. Some accidents are difficult to avoid, for example: a patient falls when remobilising after a disabling illness. In this instance, more harm may have resulted from not encouraging the patient's rehabilitation. Harm may also result from treatment, this being either an accepted or unavoidable risk of that treatment. Finally, there is always the difficulty of ascertaining how much damage is due to the natural progression of a disease compared to the other factors mentioned. These patients remain uncompensated in our present legal system.

The notion of no-fault compensation to reduce the problems mentioned above has been discussed for a number of years. The Pearson Report (1978) *in* Brazier (1987) advised limited reforms to improve the lot of severely handicapped children whether there was fault or not, but no action was taken. In late 1991, a private member's Bill to provide no-fault compensation for medical accidents failed to win sufficient Parliamentary support. Instead there is a proposal for an arbitration system to be set up that could act as an alternative to, but not a replacement for, the current system. Certainly any scheme that is more readily accessible and less combative sounds welcome.

Documentation

Under the Limitation Acts 1939–75, the period before an action for negligence can be initiated may be as long as three years from the time of the damage occurring (for children, until they are 21 years old, and for the mentally disordered, while the effects of the disorder prevent them from bringing an action). As it may take a number of years after this before a case finally comes to court, nurses' memories either have to be extraordinarily good or their actions must be carefully documented. In addition, written records are vital to show that there was no negligence as well as the reverse, and as already mentioned, any doubt tends to go in the plaintiff's favour.

As well as the documents required by the employer when a patient has an accident, nurses should be aware that any nursing records are potentially legal documents. Most health authorities now use individualised nursing care (the nursing process). Each stage of this process – assessment, identification of problems and goals, planning of care and evaluation of care – has legal implications (Young 1989).

Ward/Clinic		Cons
Surname First Name Date of Birth Address		Uni Se

STATEMENT OF INCIDENT TO PATIENTS OR VISITORS

This report is CONFIDENTIAL

It is required for the use of the Service's Solicitors only in order to enable them to advise the District and act on its behalf in any proceedings that result from this incident.

PART I	is to be completed in duplicate immediately the incident has occurred.
(below)	The bottom copy is to be sent as soon as possible to the Nursing Administrative Offices.
PART II	The top copy should be kept until Part II is completed by the Medical Officer, then sent as soon as possible to
(overleaf)	the Nursing Administrative Offices.

PART I   If patient, affix documentation label to, or complete manually, data box above. All details must be completed.
If visitor complete biographical details as follows:

Name .... Date of Birth/Age ....

Address ....

The following should be completed for all incidents:

Clinic/Hospital .... Ward/Dept. ....

Date of Admission .... Consultant ....

Diagnosis ....

Date of Incident .... Time of Incident ....

Persons Involved ....

Account of Incident ....

....

....

....

....

....

....

....

Names of Witnesses (not directly involved) ....

....

....

Addresses of Witnesses ....

....

....

To which member of staff reported ....

Name of Medical Officer informed ....

Relatives informed: If yes, name/if not, reason ....

....

Signature of member of staff in charge at time of incident

....

Figure 2.2 Sample patient accident form

There should be no conflict between legal and professional interests in the assessment of a patient. Both require this to be wide-ranging and detailed. The identification of problems and setting of goals sometimes cause concern. Nurses may feel that they are committing themselves to a certain course of action, which may subsequently prove to be unattainable. This could lead to blame in a court of law. The precautions to take here are that the problems identified are nursing or patient problems rather than medical ones, that the goals are realistic and that review dates are set which must then be honoured.

The documentation of the planning and evaluation of care is an area of potential conflict between professional and legal requirements. The professional need is for sufficient detail to be recorded for safe continuity of care; the legal requirement is not just for a record of care given but also the patient's response to that care or treatment. Precision is important, for example, in describing the response of a wound to a particular dressing regime. The importance of recording omissions of care is legally very important. For example, a district nurse refused entry to dress a patient's leg ulcers may later be accused of failing to give the patient proper attention.

Regarding the frequency of writing nursing notes, there is no legal requirement but a useful guideline is to make an entry when a review date or time occurs, when a patient's condition changes or when there is some unusual occurrence.

For some documentation, therefore, greater precision and detail are required by the law than the profession. A balance has to be struck in order for the nurse to get on with the practical component of her job but still protect herself and her colleagues in case of later litigation. With experience, nurses gain sensitivity as to what information has potential legal significance and therefore must be recorded in detail.

WNJ 576

WARD	NURSING HISTORY					

NURSING HISTORY

WARD

				Date Required	Date Arranged	Initials

Patient's name:
Address:

Telephone No:
Date of birth:
Religion:
Marital status:
Likes to be referred to as:
Occupation:

Next of kin:
Relationship:
Address:

Telephone No:
Work telephone No:

Second relative/friend who may be contacted
Name:
Address:

Telephone No:

Date of admission:
Type of admission:

Reason for admission:

Diagnosis:

G.P.'s name:
Address:

Telephone No:

Community Services involved:

Valuables:

Action taken:

Relevant medical history/operations:

Allergies:

Discharge Plan
Date of discharge: transfer
Next of kin/warden informed
Discharge to:

Transport
Escort
Out patient's appointments
Transport for Out patient's appointment
Discharge medication
Day centre attendance/Transport
Doctor's letter

Community Services

District Nurse
Community Psychiatric Nurse
Health Visitor
Social Worker
Midwife
Home Help
Meals on Wheels
Incontinence Laundry
Others please specify

Name of nurse making assessment:

ASSESSMENT SHEET
CONTROLLING BODY TEMPERATURE
Temperature

BREATHING AND CIRCULATION
Pulse   Respiration
B.P.   Skin colour
Specific problems:

Smoking habits:

NUTRITION
Height   Weight
Usual eating pattern/diet:

What help required

COMMUNICATION
Sight
Hearing
Language/speech problems
Mental state

PAIN
Description
Location
How relieved

ELIMINATION
Usual bowel pattern
Specific problems
Fibre/medication used

MICTURITION
Urinalysis
Specific problems

MENSTRUAL CYCLE

MOBILISING
What help required
Aids
Norton score

PERSONAL CLEANSING AND DRESSING
What help required
Condition of hair/nails
Condition of mouth/teeth/dentures
Condition of skin

SLEEPING
Night pattern
Day pattern
Aids to sleep

MEDICATION ON ADMISSION

SOCIAL CIRCUMSTANCES

Dependents

REACTION TO ADMISSION

PSYCHOLOGICAL CONCERNS OF PATIENT/RELATIVES

Signature of nurse making assessment:

....

Date ....

Figure 2.3 Sample nursing process documentation

Accountability and negligence

'Accountability is an integral part of professional practice since, in the course of that practice, the practitioner has to make judgements in a wide variety of circumstances and be answerable for those judgements' (UKCC 1989): so states the United Kingdom Central Council in their booklet *Exercising Accountability*, issued as a supplement to the Code of Professional Conduct. However, nowhere in this booklet is a definition of accountability given, although the concept is seen as providing a 'central focus' of the Code with its mention of both personal and professional accountability.

Sims (1967) *in* RCN (1981) defined accountability as 'being personally responsible for the outcome of professional acts' and a number of other definitions have similarly equated accountability and responsibility. The Royal College of Nursing widened the definition to link the degree of accountability with the degree of authority vested in the individual and stated that a nurse cannot be accountable without that authority. Burnard and Chapman (1988) identified that, although a nurse can be responsible for an action, accountability means being able to explain why. Therefore accountability requires knowledge. The United Kingdom Central Council has also differentiated between responsibility and accountability. In Project 2000 (UKCC 1986), they state that although a student nurse can be responsible, it is only the registered nurse who can be accountable for her actions.

The link between accountability and the legal concept of a nurse's duty of care can now be clarified. The nature of negligence supports the notion of professional accountability. A person has to have reasonable foresight (p. 28) and the *Whitehouse* case (p. 29) includes clinical judgement in the standard of care expected. However, there is divergence between the legal and professional view in two ways.

First, the law holds that whoever is giving nursing care to a patient who becomes harmed as a result will be held to be negligent. Thus a student nurse or an auxiliary nurse can successfully be sued as well as the registered nurse. (The legal position of the inexperienced or unqualified nurse is dealt with fully in Chapter 4.)

Secondly, legal responsibility for negligence can additionally be placed on the nurse's manager (Pannett 1992) as there can be negligence in delegation (see Chapter 4) and in the provision of a safe working environment (see Chapters 9 and 10). The nurse's employer can also be held responsible by vicarious liability. This has been established in a number of legal cases, but particularly clearly in the *Roe* and *Woolly* Cases 1954.

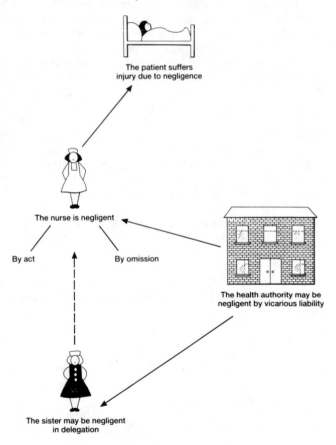

The patient suffers
injury due to negligence

The nurse is negligent

By act   By omission

The health authority may be
negligent by vicarious liability

The sister may be negligent
in delegation

Figure 2.4   Negligence and the nurse

Hospital authorities are responsible for the whole of their staff, not only nurses and doctors, but also for anaesthetists and surgeons. It does not matter whether they are permanent or temporary, resident or visiting, whole time or part time. The reason is because even if they are not servants, they are the agents of the hospital to give the treatment.

Thus the employing authority can be sued instead of or as well as the negligent nurse. However, if damages are awarded, the Civil Liability (Contribution) Act 1978 enables the employer to obtain a financial contribution from the staff involved. Although this has rarely been used, nurses are concerned that they carry sufficient insurance indemnity. The costs of litigation, which are extremely high, will usually have to be paid to the successful party in addition to any compensation awarded. Membership of a professional body or union usually provides the necessary cover.

For the employer, responsible by vicarious liability, finding the money to pay clinical negligence cases is becoming an increasing problem (Tingle 1991). Since April 1991, individual Trusts and Directly Managed Units are financially accountable for these costs rather than the health authority (NHS Management Executive 1990). Advances can be received from Regional Health Authorities or the Secretary of State (for Trusts), repayable over a maximum ten-year period. Such arrangements may lead to a variety of actions such as early out of court settlements to keep costs low and avoid the setting of costly legal precedents, to delaying tactics on the part of the NHS unit. Potential litigants may succumb to the emotional blackmail of bed closures if they bring a successful case, and may therefore choose not to proceed, denying themselves justice.

Private care

The private patient has an additional possibility of redress as he has a contract with the hospital or clinic to supply the services required. For a contract to be valid there must be:

— offer and acceptance,
— capacity of the parties concerned,
— genuine agreement,
— the object of the contract must be legal,
— the contract must be possible to perform.

This contract for services exists under the Supply of Goods and

Services Act 1982; a failure in the provision of care could lead to the individual practitioners being sued for their particular failures, or the hospital or clinic for the failure to provide the whole package of care. The private nurse should therefore be aware of her contractual position.

Conclusion

There are strong links between legal negligence and professional responsibility as defined in Clause 2 of the Code. However, the professional stance goes further than the legal one in that misconduct can occur without legal negligence and consequential damage to the patient.

Nurses worry a great deal – often unnecessarily – about negligence but it is important that they have a good knowledge-base of this subject. They can then take the proper precautions to prevent unwanted and unnecessary litigation.

References

Brazier M 1987. *Medicine, Patients and the Law*. Penguin Books, Harmondsworth, Middlesex.

Burnard P and Chapman C M 1988. *Professional and Ethical Issues in Nursing*. John Wiley, Chichester.

Medical Defence Union and Royal College of Nursing 1978. *Safeguards against Failure to Remove Swabs and Instruments from Patients*. MDU, London.

NHS Management Executive 1990. *Insurance Arrangements From April 1991*. EL (90) 195. Department of Health, London.

Padfield C 1983. *Law Made Simple*, revised F. E. Smith, 6th edition. Heinemann, London.

Pannett A J 1992. *Law of Torts*, 6th edition. M. and E. Handbooks, Pitman, London.

Royal College of Nursing 1981. *Accountability in Nursing*, RCN Seminar. RCN, London.

Tingle J 1991. Who pays for clinical negligence? *New Law Journal* May 10, pp. 630–50.

United Kingdom Central Council 1989. *Exercising Accountability*. UKCC, London.

United Kingdom Central Council 1986. *Project 2000*. UKCC, London.

United Kingdom Central Council 1992. *Code of Professional Conduct*, 3rd edition. UKCC, London.

Young A P 1989. *Legal Problems in Nursing Practice*, 2nd edition. Harper & Row, London.

CHAPTER 3

An Ordinary Nurse

Maintain and improve your professional knowledge and competence.

As was stated in Chapter 2, the standard of care expected by law is that of the 'ordinary' practitioner:

> It is sufficient if he exercises the ordinary skill of an ordinary competent man exercising that particular art. (*Bolam* v. *Friern HMC* 1957)

> A doctor who professes to exercise a special skill must exercise the ordinary skill of his speciality. (*Maynard* v. *W. Midlands RHA* 1984)

These quotations pose a central question to the unstated assumption in Clause 3 of the Code of Professional Conduct that there is a defined entity that is 'professional knowledge and competence'. That question is, what knowledge and competence can be expected of an ordinary nurse?

Another way of stating the problem was put by Burnard and Chapman (1988), who suggested: 'so all-encompassing is the role of the nurse that it is tempting to answer the question "What is Nursing?" by saying that it is "What nurses do!" ' However, this is still difficult to define as nurses work in such a wide variety of settings and even within one workplace, take on such varying responsibilities. This chapter will show how the law can give two possible answers, first that relating to registration and second the concept of accepted practice.

A registered nurse

One of the functions of the United Kingdom Central Council is to determine the rules for registration and maintain the single professional Register. Therefore, one definition of a nurse is a person whose name appears on a part of the Register. The part so specified will give an indication of the particular skills of the nurse. There are fifteen parts, as follows:

Part 1   First-level nurses trained in general nursing.
Part 2   Second-level nurses trained in general nursing (England and Wales).
Part 3   First-level nurses trained in the nursing of persons suffering from mental illness.
Part 4   Second-level nurses trained in the nursing of persons suffering from mental illness (England and Wales).
Part 5   First-level nurses trained in the nursing of persons suffering from mental handicap.
Part 6   Second-level nurses trained in the nursing of persons suffering from mental handicap (England and Wales).
Part 7   Second-level nurses (Scotland and Northern Ireland).
Part 8   Persons trained in the nursing of sick children.
Part 9   Nurses trained in the nursing of persons suffering from fever.
Part 10   Midwives.
Part 11   Health visitors.
Part 12   Nurses qualified following a course of preparation in adult nursing.
Part 13   Nurses qualified following a course of preparation in mental health nursing.
Part 14   Nurses qualified following a course of preparation in mental handicap nursing.
Part 15   Nurses qualified following a course of preparation in children's nursing.

Parts 12–15 were added in September 1989 to take account of the implementation of Project 2000 training.

It is illegal to practise as a nurse without being on this Register. A number of cases regularly come to light of such deceitful practice. An ongoing problem is of a nurse losing details of her registration. A person acquiring such information may claim to be the nurse named on the document. It is therefore important that any loss is reported to the United Kingdom Central Council who will then issue a fresh registration number. Such fraud would also be prevented by the employer checking a person's registration details before accepting her for employment, not just the documentation presented but also with the Council. An additional check is needed for the date of expiry of the current registration. This is limited to a period of three years. Failure of a nurse to renew her registration will lead to its lapsing and therefore her legal right to act as a nurse coming to an end. A person practising illegally as a nurse can be prosecuted and fined. In addition, she can be found guilty of obtaining a salary by deception.

From the patients' point of view, all this is of little obvious significance. In their eyes, anyone giving them nursing care is a nurse and their concern is that the care they receive should be good (see p. 38). Nevertheless, the legal importance of registration is the protection of the public, as a person will only be allowed on the Register after fulfilling certain criteria of training and proof of competence.

Requirements for registration

Part III of the Nurses Rules (1983, 1989) spells out the conditions within which nurse training will operate. Included are entry requirements, length of training, examinations and an outline of the competencies or outcomes required. The latter have been specifically drawn up for trainings following the Project 2000 pattern (see Figures 3.1 and 3.2).

Both competences and outcomes are worded in a broad way so that they can be applied to any nursing situation, whether involving the general or the mental handicap nurse, whether being interpreted in an acute psychiatric unit or a health centre. Neither specifically states safe care. However, the majority of the competences give a supporting framework in which safe care can be given and the Project 2000 rules refer to the responsibility and accountability that registration confers. In addition, one outcome that must be achieved – 'an understanding of the requirements of legislation relevant to the practice of nursing' – is a topic that this book specifically addresses!

Although broad wording is necessary, this still leaves unanswered precisely what must be achieved at the point of registration. Two of the legal functions of the National Boards are relevant here:

1. To arrange courses enabling people to qualify for registration

Training for admission to Parts 1 to 8 of the register.

18.–(1) Course leading to a qualification the successful completion of which shall enable an application to be made for admission to Parts 1, 3, 5 or 8 of the register shall provide opportunities *to enable the student to accept responsibility for her personal professional development and acquire the competencies* required to:

(a) advise on the promotion of health and the prevention of illness;

(b) recognise situations that may be detrimental to the health and well-being of the individual;

(c) carry out those activities involved when conducting the comprehensive assessment of a person's nursing requirements;

(d) recognise the significance of the observations made and use these to develop an initial nursing assessment;

(e) devise a plan of nursing care based on the assessment with the cooperation of the patient, to the extent that this is possible, taking into account the medical prescription;

(f) implement the planned programme of nursing care and where appropriate teach and coordinate other members of the caring team who may be responsible for implementing specific aspects of the nursing care;

(g) review the effectiveness of the nursing care provided and where appropriate, initiate any action that may be required;

(h) work in a team with other nurses, and with medical and paramedical staff and social workers;

(i) undertake the management of the care of a group of patients over a period of time and organise the appropriate support services;

related to the care of the particular type of patient with whom she is likely to come in contact when registered in that part of the register for which the student intends to qualify.

Figure 3.1   Nurses Rules competencies (from Statutory Instruments 1983, No. 873)

Preparation for entry to Parts 12, 13, 14 and 15 of the register

18A.–(1) The content of the Common Foundation Programme and the Branch Programme shall be as the Council may from time to time require.

(2) The Common Foundation Programme and the Branch Programme, shall be designed to prepare the student to assume the responsibilities and accountability that registration confers, and to prepare the nursing student to apply knowledge and skills to meet the nursing needs of individuals and of groups in health and in sickness in the area of practice of the Branch Programme and shall include enabling the student to achieve the following outcomes:

(a) the identification of the social and health implications of pregnancy and child bearing, physical and mental handicap, disease, disability, or ageing for the individual, her or his friends, family and community;

(b) the recognition of common factors which contribute to, and those which adversely affect, physical, mental and social well-being of patients and clients and take appropriate action;

(c) the use of relevant literature and research to inform the practice of nursing;

(d) the appreciation of the influence of social, political and cultural factors in relation to health care;

(e) an understanding of the requirements of legislation relevant to the practice of nursing;

(f) the use of appropriate communication skills to enable the development of helpful caring relationships with patients and clients and their families and friends, and to initiate and conduct therapeutic relationships with patients and clients;

(g) the identification of health related learning needs of patients and clients, familied and friends and to participate in health promotion;

(h) an understanding of the ethics of health care and of the nursing profession and the responsibilities which these impose on the nurse's professional practice;

(i) the identification of the needs of patients and clients to enable them to progress from varying degrees of dependence to maximum independence, or to a peaceful death;

(j) the identification of physical, psychological, social and spiritual needs of the patient or client; an awareness of values and concepts of individual care; the ability to devise a plan of care, contribute to its implementation and evaluation; and the demonstration of the application of the principles of a problem-solving approach to the practice of nursing;

(k) the ability to function effectively in a team and participate in a multi-professional approach to the care of patients and clients;

(l) the use of the appropriate channel of referral for matters not within her sphere of competence;

(m) the assignment of appropriate duties to others and the supervision, teaching and monitoring of assigned duties.

Figure 3.2 Nurses Rules training outcomes for Project 2000 (from Statutory Instruments 1989, No. 1456)

and courses of further training meeting the requirements of the Central Council as to their content and standard.
2. To arrange for examinations to be held.

Each Board draws up detailed regulations in relation to the requirements specified in the Nurses Rules. In addition, criteria and guidelines are published to enable each training institution to reach agreed standards of their courses in order for approval to be granted. These criteria can cover a wide range of characteristics of the training institution (see Figure 3.3). In addition to details of the educational curriculum and practical experience, decision-making procedures, staff establishment figures and provision of support services (to name just a few) have to be included to assist in measuring the quality of the courses. The Boards carry out these functions through education officers whose responsibilities are to advise on and inspect the trainings offered.

Part A. Matters relating to the institution

1. Name of institution
2. Educational developments
3. Relevant courses in the institution
4. Educational policy-making machinery
5. Organisational policies
6. Staff establishment
7. Teaching accommodation and learning resources
8. Welfare facilities

Part B. Matters relating to the course

9. Course details
10. Financial arrangements
11. Course management team
12. Course curriculum
13. Course content, structure and organisation
14. Practical experience
15. Assessment of competence
16. Methods for internal evaluation of the course

Figure 3.3 Application for approval/reapproval of a training institution to conduct courses
(modified from ENB Circular 1988/39/APS)

Although certain criteria must be met for approval of courses, variation is welcomed. Even within one training institution it may not be unusual for four different courses, all leading to admission to Part 1 of the Register, to be running concurrently. Even for students following the same course, the variations in clinical experience ensure that no two people's trainings, and therefore learning outcomes, are ever identical. For example, a student may not be involved in cardiac resuscitation at all during a three-year training, while a colleague on the same course may have assisted with resuscitation on a number of occasions. This means that even with detailed training criteria, it is still impossible to specify precisely in what skills a registered nurse will be competent.

Assessment, both theoretical and practical, is included in both the Nurses Rules and the criteria laid down by the Boards. One of the criteria for registration is that the student shall 'have passed an examination held or arranged by a Board – which shall be designed so as to assess the student's theoretical knowledge, practical skills and attitudes and demonstrate her ability to undertake the relevant competencies' (Statutory Instruments 1983). Assessment for safe care is central to the protection of the patient and this aspect is discussed fully in Chapter 11.

Finally, application for registration has to be supported by the training establishment that the person is a fit and proper person to be admitted to the Register (Figure 3.4). There may be rare occasions – for example, because of criminal convictions during the training period – where the institution would be unwilling to support the application, but the usual course of action would be to discontinue a person's training prior to the completion date.

With young people looking more frequently to Europe for career opportunities and experience, the status of the UK registered nurse abroad is increasingly important. To date, the only reciprocity in existence between European Community countries is in general adult nursing. Training in mental health, mental handicap and children's nursing is very variable throughout Europe and no common rules for these areas have been established.

Accepted practice

The second possible answer to what is an 'ordinary nurse' is found in the legal concept of accepted practice. This can refer to both the quality and content of the nurse's work.

United Kingdom Central Council
for Nursing, Midwifery and Health Visiting

Declaration of Good Character to support admission to a part or parts of the Council's professional register

I ....
on the basis of my knowledge of
(full name of applicant) ....

whose UKCC Professional Identification Number is ....
state that she/he is of good character and I support her/his application to be entered in the
professional register for nurses, midwives and health visitors.

Signature* .... Date ....

Post held ....

Stamp of education/
training institution

* The individual signing this form should be the person responsible for directing the
educational programme and whose name should appear on the Council's register. In
signing the Declaration of Good Character, the individual should take account of the
personal responsibilities and accountability that professional registration confers upon
those practitioners registered with the Council.

23 Portland Place, London W1N 3AF Telephone 071-637 7181 Facsimile 071-436 2924

Figure 3.4 Sample slip supporting application for registration

One way of clarifying what is the accepted content of her work is by highlighting the skills and responsibilities that are not generally included. For example, the administration of intravenous drugs may be carried out by nurses but it is not expected that a nurse undergoing basic training will be competent in this skill. This method of evaluating what nurses ordinarily do can work quite well, except for the fact that technological change can blur the division between normal and extended role (see p. 59).

In *Clark* v. *McLennon* 1983 an operation was performed to repair bladder muscles damaged after childbirth. The repair broke down and the woman was left with permanent stress incontinence. The critical argument centred on the fact that the operation was carried out much earlier after childbirth than was usual. The conclusion was that once there is a departure from accepted practice, the onus is on the defendants to justify this departure.

To apply this to nursing, if a nurse decides to use a different type of dressing on a wound and the material chosen is not generally accepted, it will be up to the nurse to justify this decision, for example by reference to research. Thus the law does not deter the practitioner from implementing change, but does expect careful consideration before departing from accepted practice.

The use of expert witnesses is vital in a court of law to state what is the accepted practice in the area under consideration. In *Bolam* v. *Friern HMC* 1957, the doctor was not negligent as he had acted 'in accordance with a practice accepted as proper by a responsible body of medical men skilled in that particular area'. The choice of expert witness by either the plaintiff or the defendant will, of course, not be totally objective. In *R.* v. *Arthur* 1981, the expert witnesses at the trial supported Dr Arthur's action in withholding nutrition from a handicapped baby (see p. 75). However, opinions of accepted practice may vary considerably. It seems likely that some consultant paediatricians would have acted in a different way from Dr Arthur if faced with similar circumstances (Skegg 1984).

Expert witnesses have been used in cases involving nurses suffering back injuries as a result of lifting. A critical part of many of these cases is the choice of lift used by the nurses concerned, as to whether it was appropriate in the circumstances. For example, two nurses attempted to lift an unconscious patient using the Australian or shoulder lift. Expert witness supported the view that the patient should have been moved by three nurses positioned in a line on one side of the bed.

The use of expert witnesses can also help in keeping the courts up to date as to changes in nursing practice. The nature of nurse training has altered over the years, leading to changes in what can be expected of the registered nurse. By their use of case law, the courts may refer back to similar cases occurring a number of years ago and this can lead to a false expectation of the ordinary nurse. A particular example of this is in the area of first aid when it is still expected that the nurse is skilled although first aid instruction during training is very limited (see p. 29). Registers of expert nurse witnesses are held by professional organisations and defence unions in order to provide the necessary information to the legal profession.

So far no specific comment has been made on the quality of care expected of an ordinary nurse. Very often quality is inherent in the choices nurses make, for example, in the comparison of dressings or the type of lift used to reposition a patient. To legislate for quality care and excellence is difficult and as has been pointed out repeatedly, the law on the whole is only concerned with safe care. However, the term 'audit' in relation to quality of care is being used quite widely. Limited legislation is possible if one of the government proposals in the White Paper *Working for Patients* (1989) is put into effect via the Audit Commission:

> To ensure that all concerned with delivering services to the patient make best use of the resources available to them, quality of service and value of money will be more rigorously audited.
> (Proposal No. 7)

Whether the linking of quality with money is to the professional's liking is another matter! However, moves are being made to introduce certain standards into the NHS through the use of the Patient's Charter (see Chapter 5).

Updating knowledge

Maintaining and improving competence are important for the quality of care given to the patient and are very rightly included in the Code of Professional Conduct. There are several legal perspectives to this.

Continuing the thread of accepted practice, the law expects this to be current practice. Therefore, keeping up to date is legally as well as professionally important. In *Hunter* v. *Hanley* 1955, the failure to read one recent article or to use newly invented equipment not yet readily available, was not negligence, but if new information is widely disseminated, then it is expected that the ordinary practitioner will read and act on this. Examples are the content of Department of Health or District Health Authority circulars and might also apply to information widely discussed in nursing journals. For example, recent information on HIV infections would influence the care nurses give and due to the wide availability of the information, this could fall into the realm of accepted current practice.

As well as the individual having a legal duty to update her knowledge and practice, there is also a responsibility laid on the employer. This is clearly expressed in relation to safety of the employee and the patient under the Health and Safety at Work Act 1974 and the law of negligence (see Chapter 10).

For example, employees should have updating in lifting techniques and nurses in specialist areas should receive additional training in the use of new equipment in order to provide safe care. Changes in documentation may occur as new theories of nursing are developed. The legal status of nursing records means that the employer again has a duty to ensure that nurses become familiar with any differences so that legal repercussions are avoided (see p. 33).

In addition to these legal responsibilities, the UKCC proposes a framework for setting standards of education and practice for all those beyond the point of registration. This Post Registration Education and Practice proposal (PREP) has nine recommendations (Figure 3.5). Of these, Nos 3 to 9 inclusive will be statutory requirements. The implementation of mandatory updating is welcomed by most practitioners although anxieties have been expressed that the minimum 5 days' study leave every 3 years will become the optimum (Shuttleworth 1991).

1. There should be a period of support for all newly registered practitioners to consolidate the competencies or learning outcomes achieved at registration.
2. A preceptor should provide the support for each newly registered practitioner.
3. All nurses, midwives and health visitors must demonstrate that they have maintained and developed their professional knowledge and competence.
4. All practitioners must record their professional development in a personal professional profile.
5. During the three years leading to periodic registration, all practitioners must complete a period of study or provide evidence of appropriate professional learning. A minimum of five days of study leave every three years must be undertaken by every registered practitioner.
6. When registered practitioners wish to return to practice after a break of five years or more, they will have to complete a return to practice programme.
7. The standard, kind and content of preparation for advanced practice will be specified by the Council. Advanced practitioners must have an appropriate Council-approved qualification recorded on the register.
8. To be eligible to practise, individuals must every three years submit a notification of practice, pay their periodic fee and either provide verification that they have completed their personal professional profile satisfactorily, or show evidence that they have completed a return to practice programme.
9. Practitioners after a break of less than five years returning to practice using a specific registered qualification shall submit a notification of practice and, within the following calendar year, provide verification that they have completed their personal professional profile satisfactorily.

(UKCC 1991)

Figure 3.5 'PREP' recommendations

Conclusion

Both the nursing profession and the law are unwilling to commit to paper a precise definition of the knowledge and competence expected of an ordinary nurse. The concept of accepted practice seems to give the clearest indication but even this is potentially liable to distortion. However, there is no doubt that the Code of

Conduct's standpoint on maintaining and improving professional knowledge and competence is supported by the law.

References

Burnard P and Chapman C M 1988. *Professional and Ethical Issues in Nursing*. John Wiley, Chichester.

English National Board 1988. *Institutional and Course Approval (Reapproval process information required, criteria and guidelines)*. Circular 1988/39/APS. ENB, London.

English National Board 1988. Regulations for the Conduct of Courses leading to Admission to Parts 1–8 of the Professional Register and Post-Basic Courses. Circular 1988/52/APS. ENB, London.

Shuttleworth A 1991. Will the minimum become an optimum? *Professional Nurse* March 1991, pp. 307–8.

Skegg P D G 1984. *Law, Ethics and Medicine*. Clarendon Press, Oxford.

Statutory Instruments 1983. *The Nurses, Midwives and Health Visitors Rules*, Approval Order No. 873.

Statutory Instruments 1989. *The Nurses Midwives and Health Visitors (Parts of the Register) Amendment (No. 2)*. Order No. 1455. HMSO, London.

Statutory Instruments 1989. *The Nurses Midwives and Health Visitors (Training) Amendment Rules*. Approval Order No. 1456. HMSO, London.

United Kingdom Central Council 1991. *'PREPP' and You*. UKCC, London.

United Kingdom Central Council 1992. *Code of Professional Conduct*, 3rd edition. UKCC, London.

White Paper 1989. *Working for Patients*. HMSO, London.

CHAPTER 4

Delegation

Acknowledge any limitations in your knowledge and competence and decline any duties or responsibilities unless able to perform them in a safe and skilled manner.

Where competence is limited, this must be acknowledged by the nurse concerned, so states the first part of Clause 4 of the Code of Professional Conduct. The following two examples will illustrate some of the difficulties that may be encountered here.

A student nurse was on her second week of her second ward placing. It was her first surgical nursing experience. One morning the nurse in charge told this student to go to the operating theatres to collect a patient who was now ready to return to the ward. The student asked, 'On my own?' and was told no one else could be spared as the ward was busy and short-staffed. The student nurse duly obeyed, although feeling rather anxious as she had not done this before.

In the second incident, a registered nurse who has been working on an oncology ward was sent to relieve for the evening to the ear, nose and throat ward. There she was allocated to care for a seriously ill patient with a newly formed tracheostomy. As she had never cared for a patient with a tracheostomy before in her professional career, she asked for instruction but this was refused. She continued to insist and eventually the nurse in charge agreed to show her how to suction a newly formed tracheostomy. However, she was not then supervised in order to check her competence.

Acknowledging limitations

There are several important differences between the two examples above. First, one involved an unregistered nurse, the other a registered nurse. As was made clear (p. 38), the law on negligence does not accept the difference regarding the standard of care expected. Secondly, an important point in the first example was the failure of the student nurse to recognise the potential danger of taking on the responsibility of collecting a patient from theatre without the necessary knowledge and experience. In the second example, the nurse was very well aware of her limitations and made efforts to point these out. Thus the patient was protected. In both cases delegation was at fault and this is discussed further (see p. 57).

Whether the individual practitioner acknowledges her limitations or not, the law is quite clear that a lack of experience or knowledge is never an excuse for incompetent care (Tingle 1988). In *Wilsher* v. *Essex AHA* 1986–88, a number of issues were raised and still await final resolution as the case is to be tried again. Martin Wilsher was born nearly three months prematurely and cared for in a specialised baby unit. Here a junior doctor misread blood oxygen levels and prescribed an excessive level of oxygen. Following this, the baby became blind. One judge adopted the following view:

> The law requires the trainee or learner to be judged by the same standard as his more experienced colleagues. If it did not, inexperience would frequently be urged as a defence to an action for professional negligence.

Another judge linked the expected standard of care to that of the post rather than the post-holder:

> To my mind the notion of a duty tailored to the actor, rather than to the act which he elects to perform, has no place in the law of tort.

Applying these statements to nursing, it seems likely that if a person elects to give nursing care, the standard must be that of a trained nurse. In general terms, the untrained or trainee nurse must give the care expected of a nurse registered in that particular part of the UKCC Register and in a highly specialist area the standard must be 'not just that of the averagely competent and well-informed [nurse] but of such a person who fills a post in a unit offering a highly specialised service' (*Wilsher* v. *Essex AHA* 1988).

Accepting or refusing delegation

Returning to the two examples at the start of this chapter, the student nurse accepted that she should do the task allocated to her; the registered nurse in the second example refused to accept the care of the patient delegated without training.

According to the Code, it is the nurse's responsibility to 'decline any duties or responsibilities' in such circumstances as illustrated. However, the contractual position of the nurse is such that she has a senior to whom she reports and who has some degree of authority over her. To the nurse, her manager is therefore seen as someone who has power and therefore a potentially adverse effect on both her immediate working conditions and her long-term career prospects. In addition, nursing is largely female-oriented and the cultural environment still tends to perpetuate the submissive role of the nurse within the hierarchy. All these pressures can influence the nurse towards unquestioning obedience to instructions.

The law supports the possibility of the inexperienced practitioner passing responsibility on to the more senior manager (*Jones* v. *Manchester Corporation* 1952). Thus the nurse recognising her lack of competence can seek advice. It seems likely that once the nurse has stated her lack of skill or experience in the delegated task and asked for instruction, the responsibility and therefore ultimately any possible blame for negligence, moves to the more senior person. Of course, if it is an area of competence that can be *expected* of an ordinary nurse (see p. 49), that nurse's contractual position may be affected.

Legal and professional actions are therefore in agreement. On the whole the experienced professional welcomes the more junior member of staff acknowledging limitations and seeking help when situations arise where competence is in doubt. It is certainly better for the patient!

Negligent delegation

A more senior nurse or manager can be negligent in delegation. Thus she may be sued for damage to the patient alongside the nurse actually giving the care. It is therefore important to know when and to whom it is safe to delegate. There are three checks that should be made:

1. The extent of the nurse's knowledge. An unusual drug regime on the oncology ward may merit the question, 'Do you know what complications you are observing for?' With the example at the start of the chapter, the least the student nurse should have been asked was what she would do if certain situations arose.
2. How skilful the nurse is in the task delegated. Again a verbal check may be sufficient. For example, in the second case the nurse in charge could have asked if the nurse had cared for tracheostomies before and was confident in doing this. A safer check would have been to ask the nurse to suction the patient while she observed this.
3. Supervision of the nurse while she carries out the delegated function. This goes further than the second point as it should take place over a period of time and follow teaching of both knowledge and skill as appropriate to supplement any deficiencies. It means managing the nursing situation in such a way that communication is good and work is planned so that staff are available to carry out a supervisory role. This is particularly important in the case of the unregistered nurse where supervision should be ongoing. A failure to supervise can lead to the nurse who delegates being sued for negligence by the less experienced nurse if she (rather than the patient) suffers harm. (This is explored further in Chapter 11.)

One final comment in this section is the issue of who can delegate to whom. As already mentioned, a hierarchy of authority exists in nursing. Its likely appearance is illustrated in Figure 4.1 and may well be reinforced by job descriptions and the grading criteria of trained nurse posts (DHSS 1988). For example, the post-holder at Scale E 'is expected to supervise junior staff and be able to teach qualified and unqualified staff, including basic and/or post-basic students'.

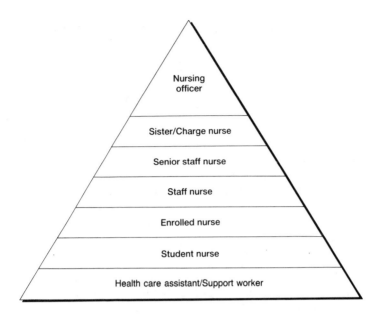

Figure 4.1 A nursing hierarchy

The scope of professional practice

In *Sutton* v. *Population Services* 1981, a nurse who failed to note or act on the evidence of a lump in a patient's breast was held to be negligent (Brazier 1987). The nurse concerned was employed in a Family Planning Clinic. This case illustrates the point that the more independent the nurse's function, the greater the risk she runs of being liable for negligence if care goes wrong. Negligence is unlikely to be shared by the nurse's manager in such a case but potentially it could be partly the fault of the doctor if he had delegated this diagnostic function to her. If it was a duty she had willingly taken on and it was seen as part of her contractual responsibility, then the blame was hers, even though diagnosis of breast lumps is not normally seen as a nursing function. The whole issue of extending the nurse's role beyond that normally accepted will now be discussed.

The debate centres mainly on areas that are normally accepted as being the responsibility of the medical staff. However, the UKCC in its document *The Scope of Professional Practice* (1992) widens the role of the nurse within the context of the changing environment:

Practice takes place in a context of continuing change and development. Such change and development may result from advances in research leading to improvement in treatment and care, from alterations to the provision of health and social care services, as a result of changes in local policies and as a result of new approaches to professional practice. Practice must, therefore, be sensitive, relevant and responsive to the needs of the individual patients and clients and have the capacity to adjust, where and when appropriate, to changing circumstances.

At the same time as the UKCC released this important new document, the Department of Health circulated a letter to inform NHS staff of the withdrawal of all previous circulars relating to defining and instructing staff in relation to the nurse's extended role. It stated, 'The (present) concept of the extended role is no longer appropriate as it may serve to limit rather than to extend the parameters of practice' (PL/CNO(92)4). The letter also drew attention to the UKCC's document, with a clear statement that 'each practitioner is personally accountable for her own practice and for the maintenance and development of her knowledge and competence'. This individual accountability, while fitting well into the legal framework of negligence, does lead to particular pressures on nurses working in certain environments.

Nursing in the acute hospital setting

Specialist nurses working in intensive care units, oncology wards and in operating theatres are particularly pressurised to carry out practices previously accepted as medical. Intravenous drug administration, the taking of blood samples and topping up epidural catheters are all examples that occur quite widely. The acceptance of a diagnostic role is particularly likely when doctors are not readily available as in *Sutton* v. *Population Services* 1981, already quoted, and in the use of triage in the Accident and Emergency Department with nurses carrying out the initial screening and categorising of patients.

The appointment of a nurse to carry out minor surgery has already occurred. At the John Radcliffe Hospital, Oxford, a nurse strips veins from patients' legs so that they can be used in a heart by-pass operation. Such merging of roles does raise the possibility of 'hybrid professionals' (Dimond 1990). Professional registration for clearly distinct professional roles may well become increasingly questioned.

The reduction in junior doctors' hours has also led to nurses taking on a wider range of responsibilities than previously, including certifying death in certain circumstances. As the Department of Health and the UKCC accept, such an increase in the scope of the nurse's practice is quite proper as long as the nurse has the knowledge and skill. It seems likely that the employer responsible for delegating such tasks will maintain vicarious liability, but it is advisable that the employee ensures her manager is aware of and accepts the need for such an enlargement in her role.

Nursing in the community

Both social and statutory change are radically altering the role of nurses in the community. For many who have worked for a number of years in the area of mental illness or mental handicap, the closure of large long stay hospitals with the move of residents into small community houses brings with it the need to develop new skills. Clause No. 4 of the Code is extremely relevant in these circumstances. The employee needs to request additional training and the employer to invest in its provision.

The new GP contracts will have a number of effects on nurses, both practice and district nurses and health visitors. Particular areas of interest are:

- a new capitation fee for GPs doing their own paediatric surveillance;
- a new sessional fee for health promotion and illness prevention clinics;
- all GPs to offer a consultation to all new patients;
- all GPs to offer an annual visit and consultation to the over-75s;
- all GPs to offer a health check to patients not seen for three years;
- two-tier targets for immunisations;
- two-tier targets for cervical cytology;
- GPs to ensure that their staff are qualified and receive training.

Such changes are creating pressures on practice nurses, as inevitably GPs are delegating quite a lot of this work to the increasing numbers of nurses they employ (Cameron 1990). Again, Clause 4 of the Code is extremely important in these circumstances. A UKCC statement in this area (1990) points out that where delegation occurs, 'the medical practitioner may retain ultimate responsibility for the patient and the practice may have arranged insurance which accepts vicarious liability for the consequences of a negligent action of a nurse employed by the practice'. The message is clearly for the nurse to check her legal position with the doctor as her employer and ensure that she has her own insurance indemnity. Practice nurses, district nurses and health visitors must also ensure that as far as possible each undertake those responsibilities for which they are best suited and properly trained. Good communication and possibly some compromise are important in these situations.

Prescribing by nurses

From October 1993, nurses are able to prescribe from a limited range of drugs, medicines and appliances. The Medicinal Products: Prescription by Nurses etc. Act 1992 permits appropriately qualified nurses working in the community to prescribe medicines and appliances needed for the care of patients and clients. Authority is initially limited to qualified district nurses and health visitors who have obtained the necessary training and qualification in prescribing. This statute provides a long-awaited and logical extension of limited powers nurses have previously taken on of modifying drug prescriptions. A Nurse Prescribers' Formulary contains the range of products approved by the Secretary of State.

Conclusion

The legal issues arising from Clause 4 of the Code of Professional Conduct can to a large extent be addressed in a satisfactory way. The one element where neither the law nor the profession can prevent harm to the patient is the inexperienced practitioner who does not recognise her limitations. It cannot be stated forcefully enough that if a nurse is inexperienced in the area in which she finds herself working, rather than risk the safety of her patients, she should ask for advice, even if this only confirms the correctness of what she has planned to do. In addition, if it is the doctor's inexperience that appears to be jeopardising the safety of the patient, a nurse should be able to take effective action in the interests of the patient. Such action should include ensuring that her concern is communicated effectively to a senior nurse or doctor and that any shared negligence is avoided (see Chapter 7).

References

Brazier M 1987. *Medicine, Patients and the Law*. Penguin Books, Harmondsworth, Middlesex.

Cameron J 1990. Unpopular practices. *Nursing Times* **86** (15), 11 April, p. 18.

Department of Health 1992. *The extended role of the nurse/scope of professional practice* PL/CNO(92)4. Department of Health, London.

DHSS 1988. *New Clinical Grading Structure for Nurses, Midwives and Health Visitors*, DHSS Letter EL(88)P33, London.

Dimond B 1990. When is a nurse a doctor? *Nursing Times* **86** (15), 11 April, p. 39.

Tingle J H 1988. Negligence and Wilsher. *Solicitors Journal* **132**(25), 24 June, pp. 910–11.

United Kingdom Central Council 1990. *Statement on Practice Nurses and Aspects of New GP Contract*. CJR/RHP/CS UKCC, London.

United Kingdom Central Council 1992. *Code of Professional Conduct*, 3rd edition. UKCC, London.

United Kingdom Central Council 1992. *The Scope of Professional Practice*. UKCC, London.

CHAPTER 5

Collaboration and Cooperation

Work in an open and cooperative manner with patients, clients and their families, foster their independence and recognise and respect their involvement in the planning and delivery of care.

Work in a collaborative and cooperative manner with health care professionals and others involved in providing care, and recognise and respect their particular contributions within the care team.

The very nature of health care dictates that practitioners from different professions have a part to play in the overall care of the patient, and in order for that care to be effective, its delivery 'must be based on mutual understanding, trust, respect and cooperation' (UKCC 1989). An additional recognition of the important role that patients and their families play in the successful planning and implementation of that care has always been an important part of the nurse's role but has not always been given the priority that it merits.

The law has long laid down the responsibilities of the medical profession towards patients and the nurse has a duty to cooperate with these. More recently, a greater awareness of patients' rights has developed, and the nurse must ensure that these are safeguarded. The balancing act between rights and responsibilities is never easy.

The Patient's Charter

1992 saw the publication of the Patient's Charter by the Government. It contained a summary of seven existing rights, three new rights from April 1992 and nine National Charter Standards. In addition, local authorities will increasingly set and publicise Local Charter Standards. The document states clearly that the ten Charter rights are 'guaranteed'. A denial of a right should lead to action by the Chief Executive of the NHS on his being informed of this and ensure that the matter is corrected. Such action scarcely constitutes a legal response. There may be debate about the objectivity of a government operating within scarce resources or the need for this route when other avenues are available and already tested.

The Charter rights

The Patient's Charter states the ten rights as listed below.

The seven existing rights are as follows.

1. To receive health care on the basis of clinical need regardless of ability to pay.
2. To be registered with a GP.
3. To receive emergency medical care at any time, through your GP or the emergency ambulance service and hospital accident and emergency department.
4. To be referred to a consultant acceptable to you when your GP thinks it necessary, and to be referred for a second opinion if you and your GP agree this is desirable.
5. To be given a clear explanation of any treatment proposed, including any risks and any alternatives, before you decide whether you will agree to treatment.
6. To have access to your health records and to know that those working for the NHS are under a legal duty to keep their contracts confidential.
7. To choose whether or not you wish to take part in medical research or medical student training.

The three new rights from April 1992 are as follows.

1. To be given detailed information on local health services, including quality standards and maximum waiting times.
2. To be guaranteed admission for treatment by a specific date no later than two years from the day when your consultant places you on a waiting list.
3. To have any complaint about NHS Services – whoever provides them – investigated and to receive a full and prompt written reply from the chief executive or general manager.

Discussion of a number of these rights and their legal implications is covered elsewhere in this book (pp. 16, 29). Debated here will be issues related to access to health care, access to information and complaints.

Access to health care

The principle behind the NHS is the right of equal access for those in need. The failure of the NHS Acts to make this principle a reality demonstrates how difficult it is to legislate in this area and the existence of the Patient's Charter is unlikely to improve the situation. Although a comparison with health care systems in some other countries demonstrates even more inequality than in our own, there are no grounds for complacency; the provision and take-up of services is extremely patchy across the United Kingdom. Sociological, cultural and religious factors all influence the situation (Cox 1983). For example, provision of an abortion service is restricted in some parts of the country with a marked Roman Catholic heritage and in Northern Ireland there is no legal provision at all as there is no Abortion Act for the province. Take-up of services that are provided varies with class and race, the white middle class being best served (Rutter and Madge 1977). Whereas in the employment area laws exist to redress any adverse effects of sex or race, the nature of the discrimination existing in health care is not readily amenable to legislation. It has to be admitted that even with the Sex Discrimination Act 1975 and the Race Relations Act 1976, the role of legislation is limited in its ability to change behaviour and attitudes at work. It therefore seems unlikely that the law or the Charter can encourage socially disadvantaged people to make better use of the health facilities in existence.

Receiving health care on the basis of clinical need regardless of ability to pay has some legal truth to it. The NHS still maintains its stance that care is free to those that receive it. Much more problematical is the notion that the individual receives health care on the basis of clinical need. There has never been an absolute right to health care. The NHS Act 1977 placed a duty on the Secretary of State to provide services to such an extent as he considers necessary to meet all reasonable requirements. As was made clear in *R.* v. *Hincks and Others* 1979 and *Re* Walker's Application 1987, it was not the function of the court to direct Parliament as to what funds to make available or how to allocate them. The court could only interfere if there had been a failure to allocate funds in a way which was reasonable or if there was a breach of public duties. Discretion has to be reasonably exercised in determining which services should be provided.

Further constraints affect the patient's right to be referred to a consultant acceptable to him. With the comparative cost of care between various provider units becoming a crucial feature in the placing of contracts, the GP and/or the local health authority may restrict choice to those providers with whom the main contracts are held (Dimond 1992). This may pose particular problems for the student or employee who spends most of his time in a different location from his official home.

Access to information

The place of the law in encouraging patient access to information about his health and illness also has some limitations. The doctor has control of the content of medical notes (p. 76) and it is he who makes the decision about what to tell the patient. He is also required to give sufficient information in order to gain a valid consent to treatment (p. 11) and there is an onus on him to give more details if the patient requests this (p. 14). However, the courts still support the doctor's judgment on how much to tell.

Under the Data Protection Act 1984 and the Access to Health Records Act 1990, information can be released from health records if the doctor considers that it will not be harmful to the patient's physical or mental health (p. 114). The precise wording of the later Act is such that it may be more difficult for doctors to block patient access to notes. From 1 November 1991, patients have been allowed application to see notes made after this date and to have inaccurate records corrected. Nurses, midwives and health visitors should therefore assume when they compile their notes that these can be seen by their patients (Tingle 1991).

Most nurses have welcomed this increased openness. They believe that they are writing more legibly and giving more thought to the records than previously. It must be stated, however, that nurses' notes were less likely to be criticised than doctors' prior to the recent legislation. Normally, notes will be released after consultation with the medical practitioner who was responsible for the clinical care of the patient rather than all of the many health care professionals involved in compiling his records (NHS Management Executive 1991).

Information and relatives

The Patient's Charter describes a number of standards and one of them is that arrangements are made to inform relatives and friends about the progress of your treatment, 'subject, of course, to your wishes'.

The nurse is often the person involved in communication with relatives and therefore she should be aware of the legal position of imparting confidential information to them. It is a frequent occurrence for doctors to tell relatives the diagnosis rather than the patient himself. Although the nurse might feel that this practice is a breach of confidentiality, it is not illegal. The patient's consent to the imparting of information to next of kin is taken as implied. If the patient does not want certain people informed, the onus is on him to inform the doctor and nurse of this. Most patients are unaware of this.

There is a particular concern where children are involved. The rights of parents to confidential information about their children was made a legal matter with the Gillick case. In 1980, the DHSS advice regarding the prescription of contraception to a girl under sixteen was to preserve the principle of doctor–patient confidentiality. Mrs Victoria Gillick sought an assurance from her local health authority that none of her daughters would receive contraceptive advice or treatment without her knowledge and consent until they were sixteen. This was refused. After several hearings, the final appeal was taken to the House of Lords in 1985. A majority found that the original advice in the DHSS circular was not unlawful on two grounds:

1. Common law has never regarded that a child cannot give consent.
2. Parental rights are derived from parental duties and these are only needed until a child is sufficiently capable of making his own decisions. Therefore parental rights are not absolute.

The nurse can therefore be assured that if a child in her care is adamant that confidential information should not be given to the parents, it would not be illegal to comply with this. However, if the child's life is at risk, or it is clearly not in the child's best interests to withhold information, the law would not prevent her viewing the situation differently.

Complaints

A woman underwent a hysterectomy and was subsequently discharged. However, after an outpatient appointment she was readmitted and had a further abdominal operation which led to a diagnosis of cancer. After several further readmissions and discharges, she died. The woman's sister complained that the hospital did not inform the woman that she had cancer until four months after the original diagnosis (Health Service Commissioner 1989).

The Hospital Complaints Procedure Act 1985 requires a health authority to set up an effective complaints procedure which has the following components:

1. The complaints procedure must be adequately publicised and accessible.
2. Complaints must be made in writing and normally within six months of the incident.
3. Where the patient is dead or unable to act for himself, the complaint can be made by a personal representative, a member of his family or some other suitable individual.
4. A designated officer who is sufficiently senior to command staff cooperation and patient confidence should receive the complaint.
5. Complaints must be investigated thoroughly, fairly and speedily.
6. All involved should be kept fully informed of the progress of the investigation.
7. Staff implicated should have the opportunity to reply.

If a complainant is not satisfied with the way the hospital has handled his complaint, it can be taken to the Health Service Commissioner (Commissioner for Complaints in Northern Ireland). The post of Commissioner is an independent position set up by Parliament to investigate complaints from those who have suffered injustice or hardship as a result of failure to provide an adequate service or because of maladministration. Where the complaint is already being dealt with in a court of law, for example as negligence or trespass, or if it concerns clinical judgement, staff appointments or disciplinary procedures, the Commissioner cannot take action. Similarly, he cannot investigate until the health authority has had sufficient chance to reply to the complaint.

Although the Hospital Complaints Procedure Act 1985 only covers inpatients, outpatients and accident and emergency cases, there are other statutory procedures for complaints about GPs, and local authorities are also required to establish procedures for considering complaints (Statutory Instruments 1990). However, the Health Service Commissioner's value is that his jurisdiction can cover the whole of the NHS and therefore can act as a back-up if local procedures fail. In his 1992 report the Commissioner noted an increased awareness of how to complain and to whom. The Patient's Charter enshrines the right to complain and it seems that the public has embraced it enthusiastically.

The example of the hysterectomy patient (p. 70) was a complex situation and ended up with the Health Service Commissioner, who upheld the complaint. He found that although at an early stage the surgeon had tried to explain to the woman her diagnosis, he had not actually used the word 'cancer', and this seems to have led to misunderstandings. He had also not recorded the fact that he had told her of her prognosis. The Commissioner also included criticism of the nursing staff in his report. He found that they had failed to inform medical staff of the patient's uncertainty about her condition, even though they had recognised this. Copies of his report were sent to the person making the complaint and to the health authority, who apologised.

A Named Nurse

The concept of the named nurse was introduced in the Patient's Charter as one of the standards to be aimed for. Within hospitals it has been argued that the named nurse finds it clearest expression in primary nursing. However, continuity of care and personalised nursing can be practised in other ways but, however interpreted, the named nurse must be the nurse who gives direct care. The Department of Health (1992) has given additional guidelines in a question and answer format. The nurse taking on this role, whether through primary nursing, patient allocation or key worker systems, should be clear of the legal implications.

First, the Charter states that the named nurse is a qualified nurse. Although the Department's guidelines suggest that this nurse may have either a first-level or second-level registration if appropriate expertise has been developed, as seen in Chapter 3, it is the first-level nurse who is trained to accept the necessary accountability.

However, secondly, in law, the total accountability of one nurse has to be questioned. The sister or charge nurse remains responsible for the overall management of a particular area and number of staff. As pointed out on p. 58, there can be negligent delegation and she therefore has a responsibility to ensure that the named nurse can safely carry out the responsibilities delegated (Tingle 1992).

A common question concerns what happens when the named nurse is not there, either off duty, off sick or on leave. Clearly the legal responsibility for the immediate care of the patient must pass to another nurse who may need to make decisions altering the original care planned. In order to avoid resentment and discontinuity, clearly agreed protocols should be in operation and, as always, good written records must be maintained.

Thirdly, the patient's right to a named nurse may mean that the patient can refuse to accept a certain person in that role. This really is an issue of respecting the individual's wishes if no way can be found around the problem (p. 86).

The role of carers

Clause 5 of the Code requires the nurse to recognise and respect the involvement, not just of patients, but also of their families in the planning and delivery of care. Traditionally, the care received by patients at home has largely been given by family members (Fry 1992). This involves feeding, washing, moving and dressing, and increasingly includes more technically skilled responsibilities, for example relating to injections and dialysis. The relatives of children and the elderly in hospital have also often been involved in a wide variety of tasks.

The nurse has to be concerned about standards when care is undertaken by relatives, at the same time as supporting and encouraging involvement. The legal position, once again, involves the possible negligence of delegating care inappropriately to a relative. As long as the relative voluntarily takes on this care with the approval of nursing staff and the care given is that normally undertaken by a relative at home, then legal outcomes should be unlikely.

Nevertheless, where the care given requires nursing skill that has to be particularly learnt, then greater consideration should be given as to how this is done. The usual rules for delegation should apply (p. 58), with training and supervision being vitally important. In addition, the permission of senior management as to the appropriateness of the delegation should be sought as the employing authority has to take vicarious liability for the nurse's actions (Young 1992).

Working with professional colleagues

The nurse works with a large number of practitioners from different professions, for example physiotherapists, dieticians, pharmacists, radiographers and, of course, doctors. Although all these relationships are important, the only one of major legal significance is that with the doctor. The nature of the doctor's responsibilities and the potential for cooperation and conflict within the nurse–doctor relationship is discussed below.

The doctor's legal responsibilities

There is no doubt that the doctor has overall responsibility for his patients, whether in the hospital or the community, within the National Health Service or private health care. There is a number of ways in which the law supports this.

First, the doctor has control over the admission and discharge of patients in hospital and the general practitioner has a legal duty to attend the patients on his list. The way in which he discharges his duties may be modified by others but the decision cannot legally be taken from him. Some examples will illustrate this.

When making the decision to admit a patient to hospital, the professional would be naïve to expect this to be made purely on the grounds of the patient's need. The availability of resources has to be a concern as, once a patient is accepted, the doctor and the health authority have a duty of care towards that patient and a failure to fulfil that duty could result in negligence (see p. 27). Supposing that the potential inpatient was a child with a severe heart condition, the doctor may be informed by the senior nurse for the paediatric area that although there is a bed available, there are insufficient trained paediatric nurses to guarantee proper care for such a sick child. The doctor would then be well advised to seek a bed in another paediatric unit. The other option would be to discharge a less sick child from the unit to make room, but the highly intensive nature of paediatric work would make this a risky decision by the doctor (see p. 126).

The doctor is also responsible for the decision to discharge a patient from hospital. Again, he may be influenced by the information he receives from the nurses involved in the care of the patient, both as to the ability of the patient to cope independently and the potential support of friends, relatives and the community services. Owing to the shortage of beds in some areas, doctors are often under considerable pressure to discharge patients as early as possible. It is vital therefore that he receives the appropriate infomation concerning which patients it would be inadvisable to discharge without the proper planning and support.

Community nurses in certain instances do have some voice in vetoing discharges if they feel community services cannot support them. This is restricted to discharges from mental health units. Consultation with and information to the patient and his carers prior to discharge is also an aim of the Patient's Charter. However, the doctor still has a decisive role to play at this time.

The diagnosis of a patient's condition is made by the doctor. Nurses assist him in this role by the observations and overall assessments they make. The experienced nurse will come to recognise the significance of these findings. Initially, she may draw the doctor's attention to items of particular concern and during ongoing observation she will recognise adverse changes that need the urgent attention of the doctor. The medical team are therefore extremely dependent on the nurses in this area, although even experienced nurses must appreciate that their training cannot give them the skills needed for medical diagnosis.

The doctor's principal role is the prescribing of treatment. This will often involve the use of drugs. The legal control of drugs lays certain requirements on the doctor. Under the Medicines Act 1968, prescription-only medicines must be supplied on a doctor's prescription (there are certain exemptions for midwives). Some examples of these drugs are tranquillisers, hypnotics, sedatives, antibiotics, antihypertensives, antidepressants and steroids. In addition, all parenteral preparations of any drug, except insulin, are on prescription only. The Misuse of Drugs Act 1971 also has certain requirements regarding doctors' prescriptions. Controlled drugs as specified in this Act must be prescribed in writing strictly in accordance with the appropriate regulations. Only rarely are these drugs allowed to be given on the doctor's verbal instructions. National Health Service hospitals often have much stricter controls than those demanded by law. Both doctors and nurse must abide by approved drug policies.

In the area of surgery, it is the doctor's legal responsibility to gain the consent of the patient. The role of the nurse as adviser or advocate has already been discussed fully (see p. 14).

Treatment or nursing care?

There may be times when it is difficult to differentiate between a particular task being medical treatment, and therefore prescribed by the doctor, or nursing care, and therefore under the control of the nursing staff.

Under certain conditions the role of the nurse may be modified to include areas of care conventionally the medical practitioner's. The nurse may diagnose the presence of breast lumps in a patient in the Family Planning Clinic (p. 59) or take on the modification of drug regimes to patients in the community (p. 61). However, the extension of the nurse's role only occurs if there is medical agreement.

More problematic is the move by the doctor to medical prescription in an area that is conventionally under the nurse's control. Nutrition and hydration are particularly involved. For example, the doctor in charge of a patient who had suffered a massive stroke refused to allow nurses to continue feeding the patient either orally or by nasogastric tube, although continuing to hydrate the patient with intravenous fluids. As the patient had previously been a well-built and healthy man, the nurses were faced with seeing a gradual deterioration in his condition over a period of three weeks before he died. Although accepting that the prognosis was minimal, the nurses were still very uncomfortable at the way his care was handled during those last weeks.

The Dr Arthur case (*R. v. Arthur* 1981) raised the same issue in a different context. A baby boy was born with Down's syndrome; the parents did not wish him to survive. Dr Arthur took the decision to prescribe a drug to suppress the baby's appetite and to order 'nursing care only', this to include the administration of water only to the baby. Sixty-nine hours after birth, the baby died.

Again this must have been a difficult situation for the nurses, particularly as the baby seemed healthy, it becoming apparent only after death that he did have some further disabilities. It was established at the trial that the baby did not starve to death so the issue of prescribing nutrition (or absence of it) was not resolved. There were some other defences (see p. 49) and the outcome of the trial was the acquittal of Dr Arthur of attempted murder (Brazier 1987).

A resolution of this dilemma might be to differentiate between medical nutrition or hydration and other more typically human ways of providing these basic requirements. The outcome of the Tony Bland case gives some clarification here (*Airedale NHS Trust* v. *Bland* 1993). The law supports the doctor's intervention in these areas of care.

Cooperation and communication

Good communication is vital for cooperation between health care professionals. Some examples already given in this chapter illustrate its importance in order to ensure the best possible care for the patient. The examples also demonstrate the overall legal control exercised by the doctor in those situations given.

The legal influences on the actual process of communication are fortunately limited. The sharing of confidential information between doctors and nurses is controlled by ethical considerations rather than legal ones (see Chapter 8) and doctors do not object to nurses having access to medical notes. However, there are two occasions when nurses need to be aware of legal implications of communication.

The first is to realise that although there may be a free exchange of information concerning a patient's condition from doctor to nurse, there are constraints on the nurse sharing such medical knowledge with the patient. The law supports the doctor's legal right to control such information and, if he so chooses, to withhold it from the patient (see p. 14).

The second occasion concerns a failure of the doctor to communicate with the nursing staff. Most hospitals have some system of recording which patients are not for resuscitation should cardiac or respiratory arrest occur. The responsibility for the decision is the doctor's, but occasionally the medical order is not recorded, either by oversight or because the condition of the patient has changed since admission. In the absence of proper instruction, the legal duty of the nurse is to begin resuscitation even if professionally she considers this to be unwarranted. Once the arrest team arrive, it is their right to decide whether to continue or not.

Cooperation in special areas

In some areas, cooperation between nurses and doctors has additional dimensions. Some of these are discussed in relation to the mentally ill, the elderly and the dying.

The Mentally Ill

The Mental Health Act 1983 defines both the doctor's and nurse's roles in several areas (Whitehead 1983). Regarding admission or detention of a patient under section, two doctors must recommend admission unless it is an emergency when only one medical practitioner is required. The nurse plays no part in these admissions. However, if a patient originally admitted informally wishes to discharge himself but those caring for him are of the opinion that this is strongly inadvisable, he may be detained under Section 5 of the Act (Section 16 of the Northern Ireland Mental Health Act). This is usually initiated by the nurse, who has a legal right to hold the patient under this section in the following circumstances:

- the nurse is a registered mental nurse or a registered nurse for the mentally subnormal,
- the nurse does not detain the patient for a period in excess of six hours,
- the patient is suffering from a mental disorder to such a degree that it is necessary for his health and safety, or for the protection of others, for him to be immediately restrained from leaving hospital,
- it is not practical to secure the immediate attendance of a suitable doctor.

Once the patient's doctor or another doctor nominated by him to act in his absence has arrived, the patient can be formally detained under Section 5. Forms 12 and 13 of the Mental Health Act must be completed by doctor and nurse respectively (see Figures 5.1 and 5.2). The Code of Practice 1990 gives further useful guidance to the nurse in this type of emergency.

Form 12

Report on hospital in-patient

Mental Health Act 1983
Section 5 (2)

(name of hospital or
mental nursing home
in which the patient is)

To the Managers of

I [   ] am

delete the phrase
which does not
apply

the registered medical practitioner

the nominee of the registered medical practitioner

in charge of the treatment of

(full name of patient)

who is an in-patient in this hospital and not at present liable to be detained under the Mental
Health Act 1983. I hereby report, for the purposes of section 5(2) of the Act, that it appears
to me that an application ought to be made under Part II of the Act for this patient's
admission to hospital for the following reasons:-

(Reasons should indicate why informal treatment is no longer appropriate)

Signed ——————————————————— Date ——————————

Time ——————————

Printed in the UK for HMSO Dd.8816357 11/83 50m 20355

Figure 5.1 Sample Form 12, Mental Health Act
Reproduced with permission of HMSO

Form 13

Record for the purposes of
Mental Health Act 1983 section 5(4)

Mental Health Act 1983
Section 5 (4)

To the Managers of

(name and address of hospital or mental nursing home)

(full name of the patient)

It appears to me –

(a) that this patient, who is receiving treatment for mental disorder as an in-patient of this hospital, is suffering from mental disorder to such a degree that it is necessary for the patient's health or safety or for the protection of others for that patient to be immediately restrained from leaving the hospital;

AND

(b) that it is not practicable to secure the immediate attendance of a registered medical practitioner for the purpose of furnishing a report under section 5(2) of the Mental Health Act 1983.

(full name of nurse) I am

a nurse registered –

delete the phrase which does not apply

(a) in Part 3 (first level nurse trained in nursing persons suffering from mental illness);
OR
(b) in Part 5 (first level nurse trained in the nursing of persons suffering from mental handicap)

of the professional register.

Signed _____   Date _____

Time _____

Printed in the UK for HMSO Dd 8816358 11/83 60m 20355

Figure 5.2 Sample Form 13, Mental Health Act
Reproduced with permission of HMSO

The doctor and nurse also have a legally defined relationship in the carrying out of psychosurgery or electroconvulsive therapy on the formally detained patient (not in Northern Ireland). For psychosurgery, the Act specifies that as well as the patient's consent, a doctor appointed by the Mental Health Act Commission must consult the patient's own doctor and nurse prior to the giving of treatment. For ECT the requirements are slightly less stringent, the MHAC only consulting the patient's doctor and nurse when there is a failure to gain consent.

It is only in the area of mental illness that statute law is used to control the nurse–doctor relationship.

The Elderly

The law is no different in this area from that applicable to younger adults. However, the implications in caring for the elderly may have an effect on the nature of the cooperation between professionals.

The equal importance of the care different professionals give to the elderly is well established and to a large extent clearly recognised by both doctors and nurses. In some geriatric units, the nature of the nurse–doctor relationship is changing. At St Pancras Hospital, the consultant felt so strongly that nurses have a valuable input into medical prescription as well as traditional nursing practice that he encouraged nurses to advise him on treatment regimes extremely successfully in the area of drug prescription. Dr Malone-Lee, the consultant, said, 'Health care everywhere is dominated by doctors and nurses have always been placed in a subordinate role. We must work towards seeing a nurse as a healer in his or her own right' (Rastan 1989). It is clear from this article that the doctor still had to take the overall legal responsibility for the patients but professional trust in the nurses' skills led to delegation of some specific functions traditionally those of the medical practitioner. Legally such delegation would need to occur within the framework suggested on p. 59.

The Dying

Much of the law relating to the dying patient is dealt with in the next chapter from the patient's perspective. However, it is worth clarifying one part of the law relating to the legality of a doctor's or nurse's actions where these seem to lead to the patient's death.

The law accepts that there is no point in prolonging the life of some patients when treatment has no useful purpose (Skegg 1984). The patient whose death is imminent most definitely falls into this category. It is then quite legal to omit care, even when that omission will allow the patient to die, or to give some care that indirectly leads to death as long as this is not the purpose of the prescribed treatment. Thus, the nurse can feel confident that the doctor is not expecting her to act illegally in these circumstances although her professional view may not always be in agreement.

Conflict between nurse and doctor

In spite of acceptance of the importance of cooperation and collaboration, differences can sometimes occur within the team regarding appropriate care and treatment. Such conflict can become an influence for good if it results in full discussion between members of the team. It may prove harmful to the care and treatment of patients unless resolved in a manner which recognises the special contribution of each . . . and ensures that the interests of the patient remain paramount.

The above statement from the United Kingdom Central Council booklet *Exercising Accountability* gives excellent guidance on professional practice. However, if there are occasions when conflict cannot be resolved, legal implications can come to the fore. For example, a nurse may decide to take on some medical responsibilities without having that authority delegated to her. A nurse wrote on a prescription chart: 'Doctor, this prescription needs altering from x drug to y, as x is not working.' As a result she was disciplined by her manager, the doctor concerned being more surprised than angry. Another situation of potential conflict is when the nurse seriously suspects that the patient's care is being jeopardised by medical prescription. In certain circumstances she can legally refuse to cooperate if she considers that negligent or criminal harm might result. This is clarified further in Chapter 7.

Conclusion

One of the expected outcomes of training (Nurses Rules 1989 Section 18A) is 'to identify the needs of patients and clients to enable them to progress from varying degrees of dependence to maximum independence, or to a peaceful death'. Clause 5 of the Code takes this further in emphasising the importance of patient and family involvement in planning and participating in care, and the Patient's Charter spells out rights and standards that could make this cooperation and collaboration a reality. However, there are a number of legal constraints to the extent to which such an ideal can be implemented, particularly in the area of patient choice.

The nurse's contribution to care as a member of a team involves cooperation not just with patients and their families but with other health care professionals. Although there are a number of legal constraints on the nurse–doctor relationship, on the whole these do not need to interfere with effective professional cooperation. However, nurses must accept that the values and perspectives of doctors and others involved in providing care may differ from their own.

References

Brazier M 1987. *Medicine, Patients and the Law*. Penguin Books, Harmondsworth, Middlesex.

Cox C 1983. *Sociology, an Introduction for Nurses, Midwives and Health Visitors*. Butterworth, London.

Department of Health 1991. *The Patient's Charter*. HMSO, London.

Department of Health 1992. *The Named Nurse – your questions answered*. HMSO, London.

Department of Health and Welsh Office 1990. Code of Practice; MHA 1983. HMSO, London.

Dimond B L 1992. Rights to health care and the role of the nurse practitioner. *British Journal of Nursing* **1** (10), pp. 516–18.

Fry A 1992. Inappropriate support. *Nursing Times* **88** (28), p. 18.

Health Service Commissioner 1989. *Second Report to Parliament: Epitome of Selected Cases Nov. 1988–March 1989*. Department of Health, London.

NHS Management Executive 1991. Access to Health Records Act 1990: HSG(91)6. NHSME. DoH, London.

NHS Management Executive 1991. *Access to Health Records Act 1990: A Guide for the NHS*. NHSME. DoH, London.

Rastan C 1989. Angels who are more than guardians. *The Independent*, 20 June.

Rutter M and Madge N 1977. *Cycles of Disadvantage*. Heinemann, London.

Skegg P D G 1984. *Law, Ethics and Medicine*. Clarendon Press, Oxford.

Statutory Instruments 1989. *The Nurses, Midwives and Health Visitors (Training) Amendment Rules*. Approval Order No. 1456. HMSO, London.

Statutory Instruments 1990. *Local Authority Social Services (Complaints Procedure)*. Order No. 2244. HMSO, London.

Tingle J 1991. For the record. *Nursing Times* **87** (38) 18 Sept, pp. 18–19.

Tingle J 1992. Primary nursing and the law. *British Journal of Nursing* **1** (5), pp. 248–51.

United Kingdom Central Council 1989. *Exercising Accountability*, UKCC, London.

United Kingdom Central Council 1992. *Code of Professional Conduct*, 3rd edition. UKCC, London.

Whitehead T 1983. *Mental Illness and the Law*, revised edition. Basil Blackwell, Oxford.

Young A P 1992. *Case Studies in Law and Nursing*. Chapman and Hall, London.

CHAPTER 6

The Unique Individual

Recognise and respect the uniqueness and dignity of each patient and client, and respond to their need for care, irrespective of their ethnic origin, religious beliefs, personal attributes, the nature of their health problems or any other factor.

Maria was involved in an accident, which left her quadriplegic. She was twenty-two and recently married and felt that there was no point in going on living. She decided to refuse to participate in treatment being offered, most notably the nursing care and physiotherapy.

Valuing the individual by taking into account his unique position and view of life, to paraphrase this seventh clause of the Code, does highlight the active nature of the professional role in relation to every individual. Maria is a dramatic example of a patient who has a particular view of life, and many other examples will be met by nurses of patients whose position in, and view of life, is different from their own. Often the differences are not immediately obvious and can therefore be overlooked if the patient is not able to express himself openly. Sometimes, even when views or wishes are articulated, the nursing or medical staff fail to respond to them. Clause 7 of the Code of Professional Conduct seems to raise two issues that have legal implications in addition to the ethical ones. The first problem is to find out what the patient's wishes, beliefs and attributes are. Legally relevant is the patient's state of mind, whether he is conscious, unconscious or in other ways incapable of expressing himself.

The second issue is whether nurses and doctors abide by the patient's wishes or respond to the patient's need for care in a paternalistic way. It may be that what the patient wants is illegal, or professionals may choose to use the law to support their own actions against the patient's views. These legal implications will be explored in relation to the commonest predicaments that nurses are likely to meet.

Ethnic and cultural differences

Health care in the United Kingdom is to a marked extent dominated by professionals (Kennedy 1981). This is a very different pattern from that experienced in many parts of the world where the care of a patient is seen as very much the responsibility of the family. In a culturally mixed and multi-racial society it may therefore seem strange to the patient to accept nurses carrying out such personal functions as washing, dressing and feeding him.

Food can create particular difficulties. If the doctor has prescribed a specific diet, relatives may circumvent this by providing their own food, with potential detriment to the patient's condition. However, legally, the patient has to consent to treatment and may refuse to cooperate. There is no legal right to compel a patient to follow a certain diet. The practical answer is for the nurse or dietitian to suggest some dietary modifications to the patient and his relatives. Customs in relation to patterns of eating and fasting should also be respected, or again the patient may withdraw his cooperation.

For some patients, to be washed by a member of the opposite sex may be totally unacceptable and for a woman to undergo a medical examination by a man may seem so alien as to be impossible for her to agree to. Again, a lack of understanding from nursing and medical staff, along with an unwillingness to adapt, may lead to a refusal of consent. In general nursing, female nurses usually predominate so it is unlikely that a female patient objecting to being washed by a male nurse cannot have her wishes respected. However, it may be more difficult to provide a female doctor to examine a female patient. With a female nurse chaperoning, the patient may agree to examination by a male doctor, but if an internal examination is required, again the patient may refuse consent. The health authority in such circumstances will not accept full liability for any resulting negligence, as the law would consider it unreasonable to expect the doctor to make an accurate diagnosis under such constraints. However, a flexible system for calling on other medical practitioners would enable the patient to make use of the resources being offered without risk of offence or refusal.

The law in relation to the general issue of racial and sexual discrimination is discussed on page 67. As pointed out, there is no specific law in this area applying to patients. What is so important for the nurse is not just the avoidance of discrimination, but the recognition of any prejudice that she may have. Only by recognising her own attributes can she effectively take action in ensuring that the patient's uniqueness is honoured. A relationship free of prejudice will assist the patient to communicate openly and make informed choices in relation to his care.

There is a further situation that can create difficulties for nursing staff in relation to family and cultural customs. Claudia Bellini had lived a long and fruitful life, with five children, eighteen grandchildren and further great-grandchildren surviving. Now she was dying in hospital and the family wanted to do as much for her as they were able, in the traditional Italian way. However, with at least six family members at the bedside at any one time, the nurses found that not only was Mrs Bellini getting no rest, but the other patients in the ward were also becoming exhausted by all the coming and going. The nurses could have used their legal authority at this point. If visitors refuse to leave hospital premises they then become trespassers and can be evicted. National Health Service premises are Crown Property, not public property. Fortunately, the nurses in this case did not have to resort to this as the family worked out a rota that was acceptable to everybody. When Claudia Bellini died the family laid her out, a last loving act that the nurses were able to honour.

Conflicting views

The example of Maria at the beginning of this chapter demonstrated the issue of potential conflicting views between professional and patient. It is in this area that the strongest emotions are likely to surface and where the law is likely to be ignored or abused. However, the following discussion will show that the law can assist the professional in honouring the wishes of the patient.

The conscious patient is usually in a position to communicate his wishes to the nurse or doctor regarding what treatment is acceptable to him. He can therefore either give or refuse consent to the

treatment being offered as long as he has the 'capacity to understand and come to a decision' (Skegg 1984) (see p. 12). Legally, it
is important therefore for the professional to assess the patient's
capacity to give a valid consent. For example, if there is concern
as to the mental state of the patient, a psychiatrist may be consulted. The nurse can assist in this assessment by reviewing the
patient's mental state over a period of time (see p. 15). These
measures might have been taken in the example of Maria.

Once it is accepted that the patient has the necessary capacity, he
has the legal right to refuse treatment even if this leads to his
death. For example, a patient with a gangrenous leg due to periph-
eral vascular disease, refused to have an amputation. He understood the implications of his refusal but found it unacceptable to
live with such an altered and, to him, incomplete body. The doctors and nurses had to honour his decision. There is a medical
argument that in life-threatening situations, patients are not capable of making rational decisions. In 1909, suffragettes on hunger
strike were force-fed against their will (*Leigh* v. *Gladstone* 1909) and
the judge held that it was the duty of prison officials to preserve
the lives of their prisoners. The conclusion to be drawn from this
was that the doctors had a duty to act against their patients'
wishes! However, practice has changed since then and the law
now upholds the duty of the doctor to abide by his patient's
refusal of consent without risk of negligence. The removal of
suicide as a criminal offence in 1961 also supports patient choice
in similar circumstances. Seemingly irrational decisions can still be
competent ones (see p. 16).

In terminal illness, a patient has the option to refuse further treatment in order to shorten his life. This may even involve a refusal
to continue with renal dialysis or ventilation if the patient is competent as legally defined. A dying patient may go further than
refusing consent to treatment. He may request that measures be
taken which actively hasten his death. Euthanasia – the mercy
killing of a patient – is illegal in the United Kingdom, even with
the patient's express agreement. A nurse administering massive
doses of insulin to geriatric patients was convicted of murder as
she intended them to die. However, if drugs are given for a reason
other than causing the death of the patient, the legal situation
may be quite different. The commonest situation met by nurses is
the administration of large doses of narcotics to control pain. As
long as the amount of drug given is deemed necessary for this
purpose, the nurse and doctor would not be guilty of murder if the
patient then died. In addition, the pattern of drug administration is

relevant. A gradual increase of the drug over a period of time would be in keeping with its purpose, whereas a sudden increase, for example from 5 mg to 75 mg of diamorphine, would be unacceptable.

There are occasions when a seemingly competent patient's refusal of consent is overruled by the medical and nursing staff. The frail elderly are sometimes put in this position. Their view that further medical intervention is unwarranted as their lives are coming to a natural conclusion may be ignored and patients may become too tired to continue to argue. As Age Concern (1986) point out, 'Dependency on others can make people vulnerable to abuse or neglect either in a family or in an institutional setting.' The nurse should remember that the elderly have as much right to make their own decisions as any other adult and should support them in their decisions (see p. 15).

Refusal of consent may also be ignored in the patient who has attempted suicide. Legally, as long as the patient was mentally competent, he could be left to die. Professionally, nurses and doctors usually feel that this is one occasion when they must act to save the patient's life. Any legal outcomes are unlikely, the patient afterwards being either so grateful that his life was saved or so determined to die that he makes a further successful attempt rather than suing the staff for assault and battery.

The situation with a patient who is incapable of giving a valid consent is rather different (see p. 18). As was stated at the start of this chapter, the initial difficulty is ascertaining the true wishes of the patient. In a number of situations it may be sufficient for the doctor to work on the principle of urgency and necessity on the assumption that the patient values his life and would therefore consent to any measures needed to save or prolong it. However, there are other situations, most notably involving those who have become permanently incompetent of making their wishes known because of 'terminal illness, serious and permanent illness, disability or severe dementia' (Greaves 1988). For example, a patient had been severely demented for several years and caused great worry to relatives and neighbours by leaving the house in his pyjamas and slippers and forgetting how to return home. One winter, not surprisingly, he caught pneumonia, and was not mentally capable of giving or refusing his consent to being treated with antibiotics.

The concept of a living will to cover these circumstances has been

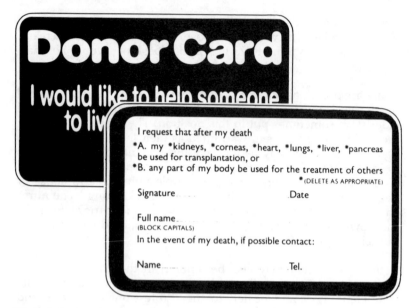

Donor Card

I would like to help someone to live

I request that after my death

*A. my *kidneys, *corneas, *heart, *lungs, *liver, *pancreas be used for transplantation, or

*B. any part of my body be used for the treatment of others

*(DELETE AS APPROPRIATE)

Signature............   .Date

Full name..
(BLOCK CAPITALS)

In the event of my death, if possible contact:

Name...........   .Tel.

Figure 6.1   Sample donor card

promoted and would relate to the 'refusal of certain forms of treatment aimed at the preservation of the person's life' (Greaves 1988). At present, living wills are not legal in the United Kingdom and there is a strong school of thought that maintains that to legalise them would create more difficulties than would be solved (Gillon 1988). In addition, it has been suggested that English law supports the doctor in ignoring life-saving measures if it can be shown that such measures serve no useful purpose and, in similar circumstances, all reasonable doctors would have acted in the same way. However, the living will can add to this debate. Legally, it cannot dictate to the doctor but it can help to guide him in reaching a decision that is not only professionally sound but also takes the patient's wishes into consideration.

A slightly similar situation exists with the donor card (see Figure 6.1). This is carried by a large number of individuals to indicate that the person would be willing to donate organs in the event of his death. Again, the donor card has no legal status, but can help relatives to make a decision on whether to allow the use of organs for transplantation, or if relatives are unavailable, the doctor or administrator who is acting for the hospital in which the patient died.

The confused or mentally ill patient may not always be legally capable of influencing his treatment, but he may still be able to communicate his wishes. Where possible the nurse should honour these. For example, a patient may put a particularly high value on privacy and as long as he is not in danger or too mentally confused to cope safely with his surroundings, the nurse can assist the patient in meeting this need. Only if the patient's safety is at risk must the nurse go against his wishes or face possible negligence.

One final point in relation to the confused or mentally ill: it is important never to assume incapacity. Capacity can vary in a number of conditions and the nurse should honour the patient's values and beliefs whenever possible. She should only refuse to accept the patient's views when it is clear that he lacks the necessary legal capacity *and* his life or health is seriously and immediately endangered.

Religious beliefs

A patient's religious beliefs may have a strong influence on his response to medical and nursing interventions. The best documented example is the effect of the Jehovah Witness beliefs on consent to blood transfusion.

In *R. v. Blaue* 1975, the victim of an assault was a Jehovah Witness. She refused consent to the blood transfusion that was necessary to save her life and Blaue, the assailant, was convicted of manslaughter. There was no suggestion that the doctor treating the victim would have been justified in overriding her refusal of consent. However, when a Jehovah Witness patient is incapable of giving consent, the situation may be different. In an emergency when the patient is unconscious, the doctor is justified in giving a blood transfusion even if he knows the patient's beliefs. The legal justification is that if the patient had known that a failure to give consent could lead to his death or grave disability, he might well have changed his mind. If the patient can foresee circumstances requiring blood transfusion, he can register his objection in advance. Thus prior to surgery the patient has the right to refuse consent to cover the operation period. Most health authorities will request that this is done in writing. If an emergency occurs during surgery, this may have to be dealt with as any other emergency when the patient is unconscious and a blood transfusion may then be given.

The implications of some religious beliefs are less well known. A patient became very distressed when a nurse removed her head-gear prior to surgery and it was not until after the operation that the nurse learnt that the patient's Rastafarian principles included a belief in keeping the head covered at all times. It would have been both legally and practically possible to have taken account of the patient's wishes in these circumstances.

Although it is unrealistic for the nurse to have a thorough knowl-edge of a wide range of religious beliefs, she should make efforts to understand the effects of the major religions in relation to diet, clothing, washing, the treatment of women and the activities around death of the patient. The recording in the notes of a contact number for a member of the religious community to give advice as needed would be helpful. It is usually possible to honour religious beliefs although some religions, for example Islam, are against post mortems and these will only be accepted if legally required by the coroner.

The role of relatives

Relatives have a role to play in assisting the nurse or doctor to take account of the patient's wishes. If the patient is unconscious or incapable in some way, relatives can give information regarding the patient's beliefs and possibly suggest what treatment the patient may or may not accept. However, they never have the legal authority to decide *for* the patient if he is an adult. There are many instances when a doctor does ask for the consent of the next of kin, either verbally or in writing, but legally this is quite unnecessary. The only justification is to minimise the risk of sub-sequent litigation on the patient's behalf, but the consent has no legal status (see p. 12).

The role of parents or guardians for a child under sixteen is rather different and is discussed below.

Children

Parents and guardians have their own values and beliefs, which will influence the giving of consent for children in their care. There are times when these beliefs will interfere with the right of the child to proper care.

In the case of *R* v. *Arthur* 1981, the doctor did not accept that the parents could take the decision to allow their baby to die by refusing consent and he therefore took that decision on himself (see p. 75). The courts uphold that in the case of a child, the doctor's *primary* obligation is to his patient. A failure by parents to fulfil their obligations to their child can lead to the transfer of their responsibilities to the local authority. Doctors and nurses will never take this decision easily but where a child is likely to die or suffer grave permanent injury due to parents' failure to give consent – for example, because of their faith – several actions are legally possible.

First, in an emergency, the doctor can proceed without consent using the argument of urgency and necessity (see p. 18). Secondly, the legal responsibility for the child can be passed to the local authority. Initially, the child can be held under an Emergency Protection Order while the paperwork is prepared to place the child in the care of the local authority. All this can take place within a very short space of time as even at night there will be a duty magistrate on call to deal with such emergencies. In Scotland, the case is referred to a Children's Panel after the initial Order, and a Supervision Order can then be made.

Another option is to make the child a ward of court when the judge will have authority over the child. Such a decision was made with Baby Alexandra, a baby with Down's syndrome and an intestinal obstruction, whom the parents had rejected (*Re.* B (A Minor) Wardship: Medical Treatment 1981). The judge authorised surgery, the decision being based on 'whether the life of this child is demonstrably going to be so awful that in effect the child must be condemned to die, or whether the life of this child is still so imponderable that it would be wrong for her to be condemned to die.' The judge was not without his own values!

A certain amount of legislation supports the child in making decisions about his care independently of adult intervention. In *Gillick* v. *W. Norfolk and Wisbech AHA and the DHSS* 1985 (p. 69), it was pointed out that under civil law the child has always been able to give consent to treatment if he has sufficient understanding. Under the Children Act 1989, the concept of parental rights is replaced by parental responsibilities only, and the child's welfare must be the paramount consideration if the court becomes involved. In these circumstances, when deciding the child's future, 'the ascertainable wishes and feelings of the child concerned' must be considered (Leenders 1990).

Personal attributes

Personal attributes may be race, culture, social class, educational background, language, sex, age and appearance. Of those not already discussed, there is little legal input.

There are fears that with the ever-present problem of scarce resources in the NHS (p. 67) the criteria for distribution of these resources may use some of the attributes listed. It is difficult to obtain any evidence of what criteria are used and how they are applied in different health authorities; for example, in the area of selection for organ donation the use of age and social background is rarely admitted but where units are relying on research moneys for their continuing existence, the selection of patients who statistically respond well to treatment does occur. As the medical profession has responsibility for these choices, open ethical debate on these issues is difficult.

The protection of children from abuse by removing them from parental control is a valid legal and social activity. Recently there have been a number of cases where legal powers seem to have been invoked unnecessarily, on the basis of parental intelligence and economic position. Considerable parental and child distress has resulted from this. However, there have also been a number of cases where a child has been left with parents where there has been doubt as to the existence of abuse. The tragic deaths of several children has been the result. The difficulties involved in making the right decisions are very real and, although the range of Court Orders under the Children Act 1989 has been widened to include special assessment orders, the need for sound professional and unbiased judgment from those dealing with children is vital.

Specific health problems

The law impinges on the treatment of some patients or clients who are potentially at risk from certain health problems. In the area of health insurance, the individual has to disclose details of any illness and information related to lifestyle. Smokers will have less advantageous insurance premiums than non-smokers and many companies refuse long-term loans to those who are HIV positive.

Pre-employment screening is a well accepted and legitimate practice. However, the outcome may be seen as discriminatory against certain groups of individuals. For example, in screening for nursing posts or nurse training there has been some criticism of the seeming bias against those with a past history of mental illness. However, screening decisions are made confidentially by medical practitioners.

In the institutional setting, various rules or policies are drawn up on the basis of promoting the health of patients and staff. Non-smoking policies are commonplace but for the smoker there may be very few smoking locations available. There is much argument as to the legitimacy of this erosion of individual rights, as there is on the ethics of providing expensive treatment for people with self-induced illnesses, particularly those that are smoking-related.

Government support for health promotion has been much publicised. Its *Health of the Nation* document (1986) sets targets in the areas of coronary heart disease, strokes, cancers, mental illness, AIDS and sexual health and accidents. However, the document will not be followed by supporting legislation nor extra finances. Its influence on specific health problems may therefore be limited.

Self-discharge

A failure to respond to the patient's needs as he perceives them may result in a failure of the patient to cooperate with health care professionals. One possible action for a hospitalised patient whose wishes are not being respected is to discharge himself. There are very few patients who legally have to be detained in hospital (see p. 21) and the majority are therefore free to leave at any time. The

DISCHARGE AGAINST MEDICAL ADVICE

I, ...

of ....

am discharging myself from..Hospital. I do this
at my own risk and realise that it is against the advice of the medical staff.

Signed :   Patient ....

Witnessed by : Sister ....

House Officer ....

Date :..

5 132 0025

Figure 6.2   Sample self-discharge form

health authority may have a form (see Figure 6.2) for the patient
to sign to show that he understands the risks of leaving against
medical advice, but there is no legal compulsion on the patient to
sign this. In the absence of a signature, it is wise for the doctor
and nurse, or two nurses witnessing the patient's departure to
sign a brief statement of the circumstances occurring.

It is useful to note that if a patient fails to cooperate with treatment
or investigations (assuming he is fully competent), there is no
legal need to keep the patient in hospital taking up valuable
resources which could be better used by others. It is quite possible
and practical for a doctor to discharge the patient even if the
patient does not want to leave. The professional view must also
be that to continue to offer care is useless. Again, proper documentation is important in case of any legal outcomes.

Conclusion

Recognising and respecting the uniqueness of the individual is
not always easy. It requires knowledge, sensitivity and self-aware-
ness on the part of the nurse. Following the patient's wishes is
not always legally possible but, apart from some exceptions, the
law largely supports the patient's right to act in accordance with
his own view of life. Avoidance of discrimination is mainly an

ethical issue and where there is the possibility of some legal control, the importance of professional judgement is still the crucial factor. However, the nurse must always be aware that the patient's interpretation of need for care may not accord with the professional's but should be valued and honoured wherever possible.

References

Age Concern 1986. *The Law and Vulnerable Elderly People*. Age Concern, Mitcham, Surrey.

Department of Health 1986. *The Health of the Nation*. HMSO, London.

Gillon R 1988. Living wills, power of attorney and medical practice. *Journal of Medical Ethics* **14**, pp. 59–60.

Greaves D 1988. Living wills; working party report. *Journal of Medical Ethics* **14**, p. 105.

Kennedy I 1981. *The Unmasking of Medicine*. Allen & Unwin, London.

Leenders F 1990. Children First. *Community Outlook* July, pp. 4–6.

Skegg P D G 1984. *Law, Ethics and Medicine*. Clarendon Press, Oxford.

United Kingdom Central Council 1992. *Code of Professional Conduct*, 3rd edition. UKCC, London.

CHAPTER 7

Conscientious Objection

Report to an appropriate person or authority at the earliest possible time,
any conscientious objection which may be relevant to your professional
practice.

There may be a number of occasions when a nurse is unwilling to
take part in care or treatment on the basis of her conscience. This
may be because she feels that it is wrong for her as an individual
to be involved, or that it is wrong for the patient. However there
is only a limited number of occasions when legally she is justified
in a refusal to participate and these are discussed below. Other
than these situations, a refusal may initiate legal consequences
that are uncomfortable for the nurse and there may be times
when the nurse feels caught between the professional and legal
requirements of her role.

The Abortion Act 1967

The one area of the law that declares the right of nurses to conscientious objection is the Abortion Act 1967 (not in Northern
Ireland).

> No person shall be under any duty, whether by contract or by a
> statutory or other legal requirements, to participate in any treatment
> authorised by this Act to which he has a conscientious objection.
> (Section 4)

However the right to object is limited in two ways. Section 4 goes
on to state:

> Nothing in the above shall affect any duty to participate in treatment

which is necessary to save the life or to prevent grave permanent injury to the physical or mental health of a pregnant woman.

A woman with a severe heart defect became pregnant in spite of taking contraceptive measures. She had previously been told that to have a baby would almost certainly kill her, so, in spite of her longing for a child, she sadly agreed to an abortion.

No nurse would have the right by law to refuse to participate on this particular occasion. Less clear are situations involving grave permanent injury, particularly when this involves the mental health of the woman. What constitutes grave? A woman attempting suicide during the pregnancy or with a past history of severe puerperal depression may come into this category; the nurse will have to accept the doctor's interpretation. In practice, unless the abortion has to be carried out as an emergency, there is usually time for the nurse to arrange for someone else to cover for her, although, as stated, she has no legal right to do so.

Conscientious objection is also limited to participating in treatment. With the majority of abortions now being carried out in the ward rather than in the operating theatre, and taking a number of hours from initiating the process to aborting the foetus, it becomes relevant as to what is meant by treatment and what would be termed other supportive nursing care for the patient. For example, involvement with administering the drugs that cause uterine contractions, monitoring the progress of these and clearing away the aborted foetus would be part of the treatment. However, keeping the patient clean, supporting her while she is vomiting or suffering other side-effects of the drugs and giving pain-killers and anti-emetics are probably not part of the Abortion Act. The practical course would be for the nurse to avoid being placed in the position of caring for these patients at all.

Acts that are potentially negligent

Conscientious objection is more than a refusal to participate on the grounds of personal belief. It may also involve professional scruples against proceeding with prescribed care that could harm the patient. For example, the nurse may be asked to perform some task that in her view is potentially negligent. As pointed out (p. 30), the nurse would share some of the blame for negligence if she agreed to go ahead with what was being asked of her.

The United Kingdom Central Council booklet *Exercising Accountability* (1989) gives two situations where the nurse might object: one involving drug administration, the other wound dressings. A detailed example will illustrate several legal actions that the nurse can follow to remedy a potentially illegal situation.

A sister was carrying out a drug round with a student nurse. On looking at an elderly patient's prescription chart, it was seen that the doctor had prescribed 0.625 mg digoxin. The sister pointed out that the normal dose was 0.0625 mg and it seemed likely that the doctor had omitted the nought by mistake, resulting in a dose ten times the normal. The sister therefore omitted to give the drug. As the doctor concerned was on the ward at the time, she went to him, pointed out the error and asked if he wished to rewrite the prescription. The doctor refused to acknowledge any error, so the sister informed him of her decision not to give the drug. However, she did not leave the matter there. As it was a common drug, she was quite sure of the correctness of her stance, so she contacted the registrar who was most concerned by the house officer's action and personally dealt with the prescription (and the doctor). In this example, the sister made sure that the patient was safeguarded by refusing to follow the prescribed treatment. Her decision was not based on medical knowledge, but on information widely known to other professionals, notably nurses and pharmacists.

The nature of the nurse's work will affect the knowledge expected of her. In an intensive care unit, a patient died because the nurse and doctor had drawn up and administered a wrong dose of lignocaine. In this situation the nurse was held to be negligent as well as the doctor as lignocaine is a drug frequently used in intensive care and therefore one for which she should have known the normal dose. The situation would be different where prescription requires a depth of medical knowledge and judgement that cannot be shared by the nurse. The nurse may query but cannot refuse to participate (see p. 104).

The sister in the first example also chose to report the matter to a senior doctor. Professionally, the nurse should attempt to prevent the negligence of colleagues. If the colleague concerned refuses to take note, the nurse can then feel free to take it further. A feeling of helplessness or powerlessness does not safeguard the patient (see p. 62) and the nurse is not acting illegally to express concern or ask advice of a nurse or doctor in a higher position of authority.

In *Exercising Accountability* the United Kingdom Central Council also discusses the importance of contacting the prescribing doctor, but if the doctor does not agree to alter the prescription, it is suggested that the nurse asks the doctor to administer the drug. Although this absolves the nurse from potential negligence and preserves the nurse–doctor relationship, as the example above shows, in certain limited and clear-cut circumstances the nurse can legally and ought professionally to take the matter further. *Exercising Accountability* also stresses the importance of documenting any incident of this kind; this is vital legally as well as professionally (see p. 33).

There are times when a nurse may feel that she has been put in a difficult position by a more senior nurse as to the appropriateness of nursing care being given. If after querying the care with her senior, the latter insists on continuing, there is no legal right of the other nurse to refuse unless there is clearly potential negligence. For example, if the nurse feels that the lift chosen to move a patient may well result in the patient being dropped, she can withdraw her cooperation. As with potential negligence involving the doctor, the nurse can only act in this way if very sure of her facts.

Acts that are potentially criminal

Very occasionally the nurse may suspect that she is becoming involved in some act that is potentially criminal. Possible euthanasia is one concern that nurses have voiced. It is rare for this concern to be borne out in practice due to the fact that drugs are usually being given for symptom control rather than to cause death and therefore the doctor or nurse involved would lack the necessary criminal intention (see p. 81). However, if the pattern of drug dosage seemed particularly unusual, the nurse could refuse to be involved if the medical staff were unable to give a satisfactory explanation (Tingle 1989).

The area of abortion can also raise potential worries of legality. Nurses participating in abortion under the Abortion Act 1967 (amended 1990) can usually assume that the Act is being followed, the main requirements being that the abortion takes place before the end of the 24th week of pregnancy and that it is necessary on the grounds that:

> the continuance of the pregnancy would involve risk to the life of the pregnant woman, or of injury to the physical or mental health of

the pregnant woman, or of any existing children of her family, greater than if the pregnancy were terminated (Section 1).

Abortion may also be performed if there is a substantial risk that if the child were born, it would suffer from such physical or mental abnormalities as to be severely handicapped.

Doctors interpret these grounds for termination of pregnancy in different ways. This is not surprising considering that the Act fails to define the degree or nature of the risks under consideration. However, as long as the doctors' decisions are made 'in good faith', the law appears to accept these variations and so, therefore, can the nurse. Certainly, to date, no relevant cases have been heard in the courts.

If a criminal act is suspected in the above examples, there is no legal requirement on the nurse to report her colleagues to the police or Director of Public Prosecutions. Any such decision must be a personal one.

Lack of safety

There have been occasions when nurses have voiced a wish not to participate in the care of certain patients because of concern for their own safety. These situations are particularly associated with caring for known violent patients or patients with certain infections such as hepatitis B and HIV.

Nurses have no licence to be selective about the categories of patients they care for. In 1990, a refusal to look after people with HIV, AIDS and hepatitis B resulted in removal of a nurse's name from the Register, with the comment that the UKCC expects all practitioners to be non-judgemental when caring for people. There are times when some sympathy can be felt for nurses who may have been put into extremely difficult situations by their managers. For example, known violent patients may have been transferred from one unit to another due to closures, without proper thought to the facilities available. Where patients with certain infections are admitted, it may be that the nurses in the ward lack the proper information and training in safety precautions. In these situations it is important that nurses voice their concern and ask for assistance and training. A failure by management then to provide a reasonably safe environment for the nurses will have legal significance; this is discussed in detail in Chapter 10. However, nurses refusing to care for the patients may well find that they have jeopardised their contractual position.

Fear of contracting AIDS from fellow workers may also produce a breakdown of satisfactory standards of care. Department of Health guidelines (1991) state that 'health-care workers who believe they may have been exposed to HIV should seek medical advice and, if appropriate, diagnostic HIV testing'. However, the UKCC guidelines (1992) suggest that a nurse who is HIV positive, 'if practising the sound techniques that should be practised in all nursing situations, is not an infection risk to patients', nor therefore to other staff (see Chapter 10).

Contractual versus professional responsibilities

In 1981, a staff nurse working in a psychiatric unit refused to participate in the care of a patient having electroconvulsive therapy. His reason was based on the Code of Professional Conduct's statement that nurses should act in the patient's interests. He was dismissed from his job as a result and lost all his appeals thereafter (Vousden 1984).

This is a particularly interesting case as it seems to highlight a conflict between the legal and professional requirements of employment. An adviser to the Royal College of Nursing Society of Psychiatric Nursing felt that the decision seemed to suggest that nurses were not responsible for their own practice. A union official stated that although the Code of Professional Conduct gives an implied responsibility to nurses to express their views when they have genuine and legitimate grounds for concern about proposed treatment, in practice they have no framework in which to express this concern.

The legal position was stated clearly by the appeal judge. No employee is required to do something that is dangerous to a third party. This reinforces what has already been stated in this chapter. However, he went on to state that although what the nurse was asked to do conflicted with *his* perception of what was in the patient's interest, this was a decision for the medical staff and was not sufficient reason for the nurse to refuse to administer electroconvulsive therapy.

Employment legislation only partially clarifies this issue. Under the Employment Protection (Consolidation) Act 1978, various grounds are given for dismissal to be fair:

- – capability or qualification,
- – conduct,
- – redundancy,
- – contravention of a statute,
- – some other substantial reasons.

Capability is 'assessed by reference to skill, aptitude, health or any other physical or mental quality' (Section 57(4)). Repeated short-term sickness or a period of long-term sickness particularly indicates lack of capability. Qualification means 'any degree, diploma or other academic, technical or professional qualification relevant to the position which the employee held'. Thus a nurse working in the psychiatric area found not to hold the RMN qualification required could be dismissed.

Contravention of a statute could indicate the loss of a driving licence due to a driving offence when use of a car is a requirement of the job. A nurse whose name is removed from the Register owing to her sickness or misconduct would be in contravention of a statute as she no longer has the legal right to practice.

Misconduct is by far the commonest ground for dismissal in the National Health Service and will cover a wide range of situations. Gross misconduct will lead to instant dismissal (see p. 112) but most instances require either suspension pending investigation or a disciplinary system of warnings (see p. 162). The initial contract agreed between employer and employee should include a reference to the relevant policies, for example, 'The disciplinary rules and appeals procedure which apply to you are contained in the Staff Handbook.' The onus for showing that dismissal has been fair is placed on the employer, who has to show that in taking the decision he acted reasonably, both in respect to the procedure used and in terms of the actual nature of the decision taken. There is now a wealth of case law to clarify the nature of what is considered reasonable (Capper 1989).

The nurse who refused to participate in electroconvulsive therapy was sacked on the grounds of misconduct. The original industrial tribunal hearing decided to uphold the dismissal on the grounds that the nurse had disobeyed a lawful and reasonable instruction. In addition, his contract of employment had stated that participation in electroconvulsive therapy might be part of his work.

A situation with some similarities to this case arose in a neonatal unit when nurses involved in the care of a baby with post-haemorrhagic encephalitis refused to cooperate in a research study (Lyall 1989). Cerebrospinal fluid was removed from the baby, tested and was then to be returned to the infant via his artificial milk feed. The nurses involved were reported as being disgusted and incredulous and, in spite of the parents giving consent, considered that they had a role to play as the patient's advocate. As the senior nurse explained, 'We failed to prove the need [of the research study] to some of our nurses who felt strongly protective towards the babies in their care.' As a result of the nurses' stand, the research study was halted.

Two differences from the previous case perhaps prevented disciplinary action being taken against the nurses. First, it concerned a pilot research study rather than treatment and the proposed research had not been submitted to an ethics committee (there is no legal requirement to do so, but it was a factor adding to the professional argument). Secondly, although the senior nurses in the paediatric area had been approached and given their approval, the nurses had not been given prior notice and therefore had not had a reasonable opportunity to voice their objections. However, the outcome of this case cannot answer what the decision might have been if taken into the legal arena.

Avoiding the predicament

There seem to be several ways in which predicaments involving objection to participation in certain treatments can be avoided.

The first is for the nurse to avoid working in areas where potential conflicts can be foreseen. If a nurse knows she would be unwilling to participate in abortions or electroconvulsive therapy, for example, even if this would involve objection on only some occasions rather than all, it would be wiser for her to choose some other area of work. It would also make the management of that ward or unit more efficient in its deployment of staff.

There may be some nursing staff who have limited choice regarding their workplace. Nurses in training or staff who have to be moved due to ward closures fall into this category. There may be some choice of where the nurse is placed, so making known potential objections may enable management to avoid placing a nurse in a difficult situation.

Clause 8 of the Code states the importance of making known to the appropriate person any 'objection relevant to professional practice'. As suggested above, this should involve management giving the nurse sufficient opportunity to voice these objections, particularly where treatment or research is likely to be controversial and not an accepted part of the nurse's work. The employer must show that any order to participate in care was reasonable.

When a nurse finds herself placed in a position of objecting to certain treatments which she has been unable to foresee, and the situation is not so clear that she can refuse to participate on the grounds of potential negligence or criminal action, she has two options. The first is to decide to face the legal consequences of refusal which may lead to dismissal. The nurse may feel so strongly on professional or personal grounds that she is willing to pay this price. The other option is to voice her objection as effectively as possible while still not compromising her contractual position by refusing to participate. Effective communication can raise the issue to a high enough profile to lead to a review of practice within that unit or health authority. The use of a health authority's grievance procedure may give some guidance on how to proceed (see p. 132).

Conclusion

The occasions when a nurse can legally refuse to participate in care or treatment are limited. Depth of knowledge and a good understanding of clinical practice will give the nurse confidence in deciding when not to take part in treatment and recognition of when her objection must take some other form than refusal. In addition, an awareness of employment legislation will help to define what is reasonable behaviour of both employer and employee.

References

Capper A 1989. *Employment Legislation*. Diploma in Nursing, Unit 2, Block 5, Part I. Distance Learning Centre, South Bank Polytechnic, London.
Department of Health 1991. *AIDS–HIV Infected Health Care Workers. Occupational guidance for health care workers, their physicians and employers*. HMSO, London.
Lyall J 1989. A human reaction. *Nursing Times* **85**(38), 20 September, p. 19.
Tingle J 1989. Medical paternalism: blowing the whistle. *Solicitors Journal* **133**(44), 3 November.

United Kingdom Central Council 1988. AIDS: testing, treatment and care. *Register*, January, p. 3.

United Kingdom Central Council 1989. *Exercising Accountability*, UKCC, London.

United Kingdom Central Council 1992. *AIDS and HIV Infection*, UKCC, London.

United Kingdom Central Council 1992. *Code of Professional Conduct*, 3rd edition. UKCC, London.

Vousden M 1984. Sacked ECT nurse loses appeal. *Nursing Mirror* **159**(18), 14 November, p. 5.

CHAPTER 8

A Privileged and Confidential Relationship

Avoid any abuse of your privileged relationship with patients and clients and of the privileged access allowed to their person, property, residence or workplace.

Protect all confidential information concerning patients and clients obtained in the course of professional practice and make disclosures only with consent, where required by the order of a court or where you can justify disclosure in the wider public interest.

Apart from the family, the nurse–patient relationship is one of the most personal there is. There is no other employment where another individual assists 'the individual, sick or well, in the performance of those activities contributing to health or its recovery (or to peaceful death) that he would perform unaided if he had the necessary strength, will or knowledge' (Henderson 1972). This degree of privilege carries special responsibilities, particularly in relation to access to the person, his property, his home and his confidential information. For all of these, the law has an input.

Trespass

The tort of trespass can be to the person, to land and to goods and all are relevant to the privileged relationship that the nurse has with the patient.

Trespass to the person has several aspects. Assault is an attempt or offer to apply unlawful force to the person of another so that the person is put in fear of violence. Battery is the actual application of force to that person. The force concerned does not have to be marked; it is sufficient intentionally to bring a material object into contact with another for this to be battery. Damage does not have to occur as with negligence (see p. 27), but there is no trespass to the person if there is no intention. Where interference is unintentional, the only redress is through negligence where there is also harm (Kiralfy 1984).

The legal basis of trespass to the person has been laid out in some detail here as it can affect the nurse in two ways. As was described in Chapter 1, a major legal defence against assault and battery is consent; consequently, inherent in the nurse–patient relationship is the careful gaining of consent to care or treatment whenever this is possible. Secondly, there are cases reported regularly of nurses who abuse their privileged position and mistreat the patients in their care. For example, a mentally handicapped patient was hit by a nurse during a party because the patient was not behaving in a way the nurse wanted. This was clearly assault and battery in civil law and may also have been so defined under criminal law (see p. 152). In addition, the nurse was found guilty of professional misconduct and had her name removed from the Register (see p. 5).

Trespass to land involves an interference with the possession of land. Thus, even if a house is not owned by the resident, but this person has possession, then he has the right to sue anybody who is unlawfully there. Trespass may involve unauthorised entry or unauthorised remaining on land after somebody has been asked to leave (see p. 119). Some individuals – for example, the police – have certain rights of entry and these are clearly laid down by law, but nurses have no such rights. The position of the nurse in the community is discussed on p. 113. Trespass to land is not a criminal offence.

Wrongful interference to goods can also be trespass and is again a wrong against possession. In law, possession is linked to control and an intention to exclude others from this possession. The issue of how the nurse deals with patients' property, therefore, has a legal component under this part of the law. In addition, negligence and criminal law are also relevant and are included in the discussion below.

Personal property

When a patient in hospital is unable to take responsibility for his belongings, the nurse has to ensure that both her own and the patient's rights are taken into account.

The commonest example is when a patient is unconscious. The nurse in this situation becomes an involuntary bailee. This means that she must take as much care of the property as the patient would if he were able. The patient who is confused or under the influence of alcohol or drugs is in a similar category.

A young man was brought into the Accident and Emergency Department with lacerations to his face. He was drunk and unable to stand unaided for more than a few seconds. Two nurses therefore decided it was necessary to check his belongings for valuables. They checked his clothing together and found a wallet containing several credit cards and some loose change amounting to approximately five pounds. He also had a ring on his finger and a chain around his neck. They made a list of his property and an additional signed list of his valuables, noting down details of a yellow metal ring and a yellow metal chain, before locking these in a safe. Thirty minutes later, the patient accused the nurses of stealing his property and although partially reassured on being shown the list, still insisted he had had a further twenty pounds that had not been recorded. He became abusive to the nurses and complained to a police officer who happened to be present in the Department.

In this example, the nurses were quite correct in taking on the responsibility for the patient's property. The care with which they carried this out was also to protect them legally in case of later accusations of theft. Thus the two were witnesses of each other's actions. The description of the valuables also protects the nurses and health authority in case of later loss of these items; thus 'yellow metal' is stated rather than gold. In a dispute over compensation for any loss, the health authority would not necessarily have to pay out the cost of a gold ring where the description was merely of yellow metal (Young 1989). Nurses have commented that this does seem rather unfair to the patient with a genuine claim, but it is a ruling that they are required to follow.

Theft is a serious crime and the police officer involved in the example above would probably be required to follow it up. The patient's property may well be checked a second time in case money has been overlooked. The nurses involved in the incident would be asked to make statements of what had occurred (see p. 117), including any periods of time when the property was left unattended. This underlines the importance of checking property as soon after admission or reception as possible to protect both the patient and the nurse. In addition, during transfer of patients from one area to another and the period when a patient is undergoing investigations or is under general anaesthesia, adequate precautions must be taken to safeguard property. If property is lost in situations where it has been difficult for the patient to retain full control over it, the health authority may well find itself liable for negligence in spite of disclaimers often made to the contrary.

Very occasionally an accusation of theft is upheld. For theft to be proved, it must be shown that the offender intends permanently to deprive the owner of the property. Some nurses do not see the 'borrowing' of hospital property as theft on this basis, for example using bed linen from the ward which will then be returned when it needs laundering. However, the employer will see both theft and unauthorised borrowing as gross misconduct and instant dismissal will result.

The police can prosecute a nurse for theft although sometimes the patient is unwilling to press charges, particularly if his property has been returned to him. However, if the case goes to court, an order can be made for the restoration of stolen property to its owner. The nurse should also be aware that any convictions are automatically reported to her statutory body so that the nurse may also have a case to answer to the Professional Conduct Committee (see p. 4).

The fully conscious patient can expect his right of control over his belongings not to be questioned. The nurse can offer to lock up any valuables for safekeeping but cannot insist and if the patient refuses this offer, having been warned of the risks, he cannot hold the health authority responsible for any loss. The same rules apply were the patient brings his own drugs into hospital. Professionally, the nurse may be concerned that it is potentially dangerous for patients to keep their previously prescribed medicines in case the doctor is not then informed of these and the drugs may adversely affect new prescriptions. However, the law is clear on ownership of these medicines.

There is one occasion when the nurse must remove a patient's property from him to prevent a worse wrong.

A patient was admitted as an emergency under Section 4 of the Mental Health Act. She had attempted suicide and was still in a distraught state of mind. When the nurses asked to go through her belongings she refused, but the nurses explained that they had a duty to do so. The reason was to check if she had on her any means of killing herself, for example, tablets, razor blades, a long scarf or belt. If this check had not been made and the patient had then committed suicide, the nurses would have been held negligent, knowing that the patient was at risk.

Patients' homes

There is a certain amount of legislation that protects both the patient and the nurse when the care takes place in the patient's home. The tort of trespass protects the patient. The nurse has no right of entry into a patient's home however great the need and if at any time she is asked to leave, she must do so or become a trespasser. It is important that the nurse documents any failure to gain access to a patient in case of later accusations of her failing to carry out her duties properly (see p. 35). Sometimes a patient who is bedridden will offer to give a front door key to the nurse. She would be wise to refuse, again in case of later accusations of unlawful entry. In such a situation, the nurse could suggest that the key be left with a neighbour for her to collect. Occasionally a nurse, on receiving no answer to the doorbell, may be so concerned as to the health of her patient that she is tempted to force an entry to check. Such an act, while being motivated by the best intentions, is illegal. In this event she should contact the police who can then make the appropriate decision.

The community nurse is also protected by the law to some extent. There are particular difficulties and dangers that she faces from potentially unsafe surroundings and even from abusive relatives. The employer's responsibilities in these circumstances are discussed in the next chapter, but under the Occupiers' Liability Acts 1957 and 1984, the occupier must ensure that he takes reasonable measures to protect the safety of anyone on his premises (see p. 141). For example, a nurse falling down stairs due to the banister being rotten would have grounds for complaint. A district nurse visiting an elderly lady always refused to enter the house until the three large dogs inside had been securely locked in another room. Another nurse similarly refused to enter a patient's home when the woman's husband was present as he had attempted to assault her on one occasion and has been verbally abusive on several others. In both situations, the patients responded to the nurses' very proper stance and thus the nurses avoided damage and the patients avoided litigation. Even if the nurse had been trespassing, the occupier still has a responsibility to warn of potential dangers: for example, dangerous dogs.

The law and confidential information

A major concern for nurses is the handling of confidential information both from and about their patients. Considering the importance of this area of the professionals' work, it is surprising that legislation has only recently been placed in the statute books to cover some aspects of confidentiality.

In Scotland, a breach of confidence is covered by the law of torts. A person who stands in a confidential relationship with another can be sued if a breach of that confidence results in injury. However, in England, Wales and Northern Ireland, the only route that can be taken is for the patient to sue the nurse for defamation (see p. 3). For several reasons this is impractical and unlikely to succeed. First, the material has to be of such a nature that the person is lowered in the eyes of 'right thinking' people. In the past, allegations of venereal disease or immorality would have been put into this category. However, a major defence is that the defamatory material is true. This usually prevents successful actions being taken unless the purpose of the breach was to bring the patient into disrepute. A second difficulty is the cost of taking legal action. As defamation cases are not covered by legal aid, this in practice rules out all but the very affluent from taking action.

While oral and some written information remains relatively free of direct legal control, written records concerning patients or clients are subject to a number of controls. While the main purpose of the law is to provide certain rights of access to information (p. 70), the requirements spelt out also ensure that access is limited to those entitled to it. The Access to Health Records Act 1990, the Access to Personal Files Act 1987 relating to Social Services files, and the Access to Medical Reports Act 1988 relating to medical information provided for employment or insurance purposes, are all relevant statutes.

Automatically processed data is covered by the specific rules of the Data Protection Act 1984. The use of computers is becoming rapidly more widespread in health care. Nurses in a number of areas are being required both to input and access information about their patients for a number of purposes, for example health screening, medical appointments and staffing levels (see p. 128). It is therefore important that nurses understand the implications of this Act in order to function within the law. In addition, an employee is personally liable under the Act for damage caused by inadequate security of personal data and the employer will not necessarily pay on her behalf any compensation ordered.

Included in Schedule 1 of the Data Protection Act are eight principles. These are that personal data are:

1. obtained fairly and lawfully,
2. held only for one or more lawful purposes specified in the data user's register entry (an important requirement of the Act is registration by applying to an independent Data Protection Registrar),
3. used or disclosed only in accordance with the data user's register entry,
4. adequate, relevant and not excessive for these purposes,
5. accurate and where necessary up to date,
6. not kept longer than is necessary for the specified purpose,
7. made available to data subjects on request,
8. properly protected against loss or disclosure.

For the nurse a number of relevant details arise from these principles. The use and disclosure of information will be on a similar but legal basis compared to other more conventional records. It should only be shared with other professionals directly involved with the patients and to the staff particularly concerned with managing the area. Subject data being entered should only cover information necessary for the purpose for which it is gathered. For example, in a health screening for cervical cancer only medical history that is directly relevant should be recorded, such as any previous suspicious smears, not a tonsillectomy twenty years ago!

Accuracy of data can be checked by giving the data subject a printout, but this may not be possible with patients. This is because personal health data are covered by a specific exemption clause so that although a patient may request to have access to the information, the doctor may refuse to divulge any or all of this on the grounds that it may be harmful to the patient's physical or mental health. Similar restrictions apply to written records under the Access to Health Records Act 1990.

Finally, great care must be taken to protect confidentiality. From the nurse's point of view this means that:

- all equipment should be sited in a secure location not vulnerable to vandalism or theft,
- visual display units and printers should be sited so they cannot be seen by members of the public or unauthorised staff,
- a system of limited access should be in operation, using privilege levels and passwords,
- clear back-up procedures should be established in case of accidental loss or damage,
- obsolete data should be erased,
- strict procedures for the distribution, storage and disposal of printed output should be established,
- if unauthorised disclosure is suspected, the local data protection officer should be informed.

It is also important that the nurse realises that the Computer Misuse Act 1990 makes some types of unauthorised access a criminal offence.

When disclosure is required

There are occasions when the law requires or supports the disclosure of confidential information. The nurse's position in relation to the courts, the police and the employer is considered below.

Confidential material is not subject to privilege in the courts. A court can order information to be released following a request from anyone involved in a legal action, but the court decides the details of what should be released. In Scotland, access to the medical or nursing records can be offered to an independent medical expert of the patient's choice if the original doctor does not object or, if he does object, the court can order their production.

A nurse acting as a witness must disclose information to the court if required to do so. Prior to appearing in court, it is advisable to talk over the case with her legal representative in order to rehearse the material to be presented and to make some predictions of the questions that the nurse may face during cross-examination. When giving evidence, the nurse should attempt to preserve confidentiality as far as possible by giving the minimal information required for the case being heard. She must keep to the facts and avoid inferences and opinions. She is allowed to refer to relevant records made by herself as long as those were made at or shortly after the event recorded, but she must be aware that any written material used must be made available to the court if required. If a witness becomes flustered during examination, there is the danger that she may divulge more information than she intends. It is therefore important that the nurse remains calm, gives herself time to retain her composure if she feels herself becoming angry or overanxious and, if unsure, asks for questions to be repeated or rephrased.

There are occasions when the police ask the nurse to divulge confidential information, but the nurse must be clear that they have no legal right to demand this. The police do not necessarily make it easy for the nurse to refuse, but she should bear in mind that they are only doing a job that is often far from easy and she should remain polite but firm in her refusal. If necessary she should refer the police to her manager or the doctor if it is a question concerning diagnosis. There may be times when the nurse decides it is in the patient's interests to divulge some information, for example to remove doubts over a patient's possible illegal actions. The reverse situation may also lead the nurse to speak to the police. Clause 9 of the Code of Professional Conduct accepts that breach of confidentiality may be necessary 'in the public interest'. It is extremely difficult for the nurse to decide what situations may fall within this category. Some examples may be the finding of a lethal weapon or large quantities of addictive drugs on an unconscious person brought to the Accident and Emergency Department. The United Kingdom Central Council Advisory Paper on confidentiality states 'that the responsibility to either disclose or withhold confidential information in the public interest lies with the individual practitioner, that she cannot delegate the decision and that she cannot be required by a superior to disclose or withhold information against her will' (UKCC 1987). The nurse divulging such information will be asked by the police to make a statement. In this, as in other circumstances where a statement is required, the nurse should again be aware that the making of a statement is entirely voluntary. She should also be aware that no individual can be required to go to a police station in order to make a statement; forcing an individual to accompany the police to the police station cannot take place unless the individual is arrested.

A last situation where a nurse may be asked to divulge confidential information involves employment legislation. A nurse going off sick is required to inform her manager, who may ask what the nature of the illness is. In fact, there is no compulsion on the sick employee to divulge this, but the employer is allowed to ask for some indication of how long the sickness is likely to last. The occupational health nurse may be asked to review the sickness pattern of an employee by the relevant manager. Again, the Occupational Health Department cannot be required to divulge details of the employee's sickness but must give an indication of the future likelihood of the employee either returning to work or having a much improved sickness record. Any further details can only be disclosed with the consent of the employee.

Preventing disclosure

As has been seen, there is little in the law that specifically prevents breach of confidentiality. However, there are two other areas of the law that can be used.

An employer can have a specific policy regarding confidentiality. The Confidentiality Working Group of the DHSS Steering Group on Health Services Information (UKCC 1987) suggested a form of words that can be used; part of this is quoted below:

> In the course of your duties you may have access to confidential matter about patients, members of staff or other health service business. On no account must information relating to identifiable patients be divulged to anyone other than authorised persons, for example medical, nursing or other professional staff as appropriate, who are concerned directly with the care, diagnosis and/or treatment of the patient. . . . Failure to observe these rules will be regarded by your employers as serious misconduct which could result in serious disciplinary action being taken against you, including dismissal.

The employee is usually required to sign that she has had these rules explained to her and that she has understood them. However, although the possibility of discipline then exists, it may be difficult to enforce. Breach of confidentiality is often unintentional and occurs away from the place of work. For example, two nurses on their way home by public transport may be chatting about their patients. Although they may be overheard, it is unlikely that there would be any obvious outcome, even if the patients' names were recognised by a fellow passenger. At least the inclusion of confidentiality within the nurse's contract does underline its importance.

There is one other route that the patient can use to prevent disclosure. An injunction is a court order requiring or prohibiting the doing of a particular act (Pritchard 1982). Most injunctions are prohibitory and in this case could prevent the sharing of confidential information beyond the immediate professionals and administrators concerned with a person's hospitalisation.

An injunction is granted by a court. The court has discretion to refuse unless the case is a meritorious one and the applicant has acted properly. If the matter is urgent, which may well apply in cases of sickness and hospitalisation, the court may grant a temporary injunction without having to hear the other side. A failure to abide by an injunction is contempt of court and carries the possible penalty of fines or even imprisonment. Compensation for damages is rarely considered to be a useful remedy as the whole reason for using this particular legal process is the lack of redress by suing in the civil courts.

In practice the use of injunctions to prevent breach of confidentiality is limited. The famous are often concerned to maintain privacy over their health matters and therefore may see the injunction as a useful tool. But as with any legal process, there is a cost.

An additional threat to privacy is the unwelcome invasion of hospital property by the press or members of the public. Patients usually have to rely on the discretion of hospital staff to use the law on trespass (see p. 110) to evict any particularly insistent members of the press or public who attempt to gain access to them or the staff involved in their care, without their permission. Nurses may need to call on security staff or the police for assistance.

Conclusion

The law gives some protection to both patient and nurse within the context of the special privileges existing between them. Where property is concerned, both common and statute law provide remedies against abuse. It is in the area of information that the role of the law is limited. Although there are some legal frameworks which can be used to support either the keeping or the disclosure of confidential information, professional decisions have to be made on the whole on the basis of ethical considerations. In this area, the rights of the patient are limited and even recent legislation leaves control with the professional rather than passing it to the individual to whom it is of most concern.

References

Henderson V 1972. *Basic Principles of Nursing Care*. International Council of Nurses, Geneva.

Kiralfy A K R 1984. *The English Legal System*, 7th edition. Sweet & Maxwell, London.

Pritchard J 1982. *The Penguin Guide to the Law*. Penguin Books, Harmondsworth, Middlesex.

United Kingdom Central Council 1987. *Confidentiality*, Advisory Paper. UKCC, London.

United Kingdom Central Council 1992. *Code of Professional Conduct*, 3rd edition. UKCC, London.

Young A P 1989. *Legal Problems in Nursing Practice*, 2nd edition. Harper & Row, London.

CHAPTER 9

The Environment of Care

Report to an appropriate person or authority, having regard to the physical, psychological and social effects on patients and clients, any circumstances in the environment of care which could jeopardise standards of practice.

Report to an appropriate person or authority any circumstances in which safe and appropriate care for patients and clients cannot be provided.

During an influenza epidemic, in one week one third of the staff were off sick in a long-stay geriatric ward. There was no chance of moving nurses from other wards as they were similarly affected, no likelihood of employing agency staff in this epidemic and no possibility of sending any of the patients home. The only option was to review the workload and decide on the priorities of care that needed to be given to maintain safety. For example, the majority of the patients had to stay in bed and a rota was worked out so that each patient had a thorough wash once a week and on other days only essential hygiene needs were carried out. Morale of staff and patients remained surprisingly high as the patients on the whole appreciated that this was short-term and some even enjoyed the extra rest! For their part, the nurses were able to cope with the work and, in this limited period, no patients came to any harm.

The setting in which nursing takes place is crucial to the care that patients receive. This 'environment of care', as Clause 11 of the Code of Professional Conduct calls it, must be supported by sufficient resources in order for safety to be maintained. As illustrated in the example above, there are times when this is difficult and, as staff levels are pared down to a minimum in these cost-conscious times, such crises are likely to occur more frequently. As pointed out in the Code, the environment of care can have physical, psychological and social effects on patients and clients. This chapter will look at a number of facets of the environment as well as addressing the contentious issue of reporting to 'an appropriate person or authority'.

The physical environment

The nurse will be concerned with a number of aspects of the physical environment that have legal controls. The giving of safe care is influenced by size, layout, stairways, lifts, lighting, ventilation and temperature. Since the lifting of Crown immunity, a number of controls are now applicable to NHS property that hitherto were not required. The NHS and Community Care Act 1990 provided for the removal of Crown immunity from a large number of statutes although previously food hygiene, health and safety and radioactive substances legislation had been freed from this immunity. As the implications are quite major, transitional arrangements are having to be applied, for example, where building work was under way at the time of the statute becoming law (DoH 1990). Building Regulations under the Building Act 1984 and the Town and Country Planning Act 1990 ensure that any buildings, whether new or requiring alteration, abide by certain standards set and checked by the local authority. Control of the use of incinerators is required under the Environment Protection Act 1990 and of other waste disposal by the Control of Pollution Act 1974.

The nurse may notice that as such controls are implemented the physical environment shows some improvement, but such changes will be slow, not being retroactively applied on current buildings unless under the remit of fire precautions.

Fire

The most important legislation relating to fire prevention is the Fire Precautions Act 1971 (and as amended by the Fire Safety and Safety of Places of Sport Act 1987). A fire certificate has to be issued to large premises designated for certain purposes and the criteria for its issue are stringent and particularly consider:

1. means of escape which include clearly visible and properly

illuminated fire exits and emergency lighting throughout escape routes;

2. means for fighting fire including hand extinguishers and fixed appliances such as hoses;
3. means to give warning in case of fire, that is fire alarm systems which may include smoke and heat detection systems.

If the fire authority is not satisfied with the points listed above, it may refuse to issue a fire certificate. Any owner or employer would be ill advised to continue to operate in such circumstances (Beckett and Young 1989).

The difficulty in relation to the NHS is that only a limited number of premises will fall within the statutory remit of requiring a fire certificate. The legislation only applies to factories, offices, shops and railway premises over a certain size and hotels and boarding houses where accommodation is provided for more than six people. There are no regulations specifically applying the Act to hospital wards and patients.

In nursing and residential homes, full statutory fire precautions can be enforced. In addition, non-health service hospitals, homes and clinics have always been under the control of Building Regulations under which the design and construction of buildings to reduce the risk of fire must be approved. This involves the use of specified materials that are fire resistant and the careful positioning of doors and stairwells.

In the situation of property being outside the requirement for a fire certificate, the local fire authority does have some powers under the 1971 Act to prohibit or to restrict the use of any premises occupied by health service bodies and NHS Trusts where they consider there is 'a serious risk to persons in the event of fire'. In addition, the employer still has a duty under the Health and Safety at Work Act 1974 and civil law but this lacks the precision required by a fire certificate.

It is important that nurses take particular note of the following. Escape routes must be available and free of obstruction at all times. This seems to be particularly difficult to maintain as unwanted equipment and beds, rubbish bags and dirty linen bags awaiting collection seem to accumulate at just such points. Fire-resisting doors must be kept closed in order to keep fire localised. Often these are found propped open when they hinder the passage of large numbers of people or where ventilation is poor. Nurses have a duty to attempt to remedy these dangerous practices themselves and by informing their manager, their safety representatives or the fire prevention officer if there is one employed by the health authority.

Staff training is vitally important but is rarely carried out effectively. An employer must document that training has been given but this is usually minimal, for example two to three hours only. Although staff are shown how to operate fire extinguishers, there are rarely the resources to enable all nurses to become confident in handling these. Fire drills are also an important part of training. These tend to be carried out infrequently, if at all, in patient areas. Usually, drills involving the wards are carried out with prior notice. Evacuation techniques can be practised on other staff but feel very different when involving the ill and immobile being moved from a ward to a designated safe area.

Other responsibilities all employers should carry out are testing of fire alarm systems on a regular and frequent basis and checking on the availability and good working order of any fire-fighting equipment.

Nurses may be involved in one further fire hazard. A problem can occur if a patient of diminished responsibility repeatedly calls the Fire Brigade. Under the Fire Services Act 1947–59, legal action can be taken against a person who makes a 999 call if it proves to be a false alarm and was made with malicious intent. Taking this further, it is not unknown for a disturbed patient to cause a fire. In both circumstances the nurse must accept some responsibility for failing to supervise the patient properly, but these types of situation are always dealt with sympathetically by both the Fire Brigade and the police.

Infections

Patients in hospital are likely to be particularly susceptible to infections due to the fact that they are already ill or undergoing surgery. Although a number of deaths occur due to secondary infection, it is only occasionally that public attention is caught, for example by the deaths of critically ill babies following MRSA infection (a particularly virulent and resistant bacteria). More often, a patient's stay in hospital is prolonged and recovery delayed by a hospital-acquired infection.

The poor history of building maintenance in the NHS and inadequate toilet and washing facilities for patients and staff do not promote an environment with few bacteria, viruses and unwanted pests. A failure by the employer to take reasonable measures can lead to an action for negligence. This may bring some pressure to bear to take more positive steps. Proper training in infection control is now being seen as important as well as cost effective. The lifting of Crown immunity from food hygiene legislation is likely to have a marked influence in reducing food poisoning in both patients and staff. Hospital kitchens have already been closed by safety inspectors and health authorities successfully prosecuted.

A major problem for anyone undertaking nursing in the National Health Service is the conflict between maintaining good standards of care and only taking on what is a reasonable workload as an individual. A number of studies has been carried out to determine why nurses leave nursing; one fairly frequently mentioned reason given is the conflict between the actual and the ideal which many individuals cannot resolve. For some, sooner or later the frustration becomes too intense for them to remain in nursing.

The law is only marginally concerned with the effect of all this on nurses although employment legislation can give some protection to the nurse working under pressure. However, the law on negligence once again plays a key part in as much as nurses too hard-pressed can make mistakes which in turn harm patients. Both manager and clinical nurse can use knowledge of this to protect both themselves and the patients.

Management responsibility

The health authority is directly liable for providing the patient with 'reasonably careful, competent and skilled care and treatment' once he has been admitted (Lord Denning). This has to be of concern to the doctor when he is considering the need to admit a patient as an emergency (see p. 73) and to the hospital administrator as to how many patients on the waiting-list to call in for surgery (Brazier 1987).

The nurse manager is in a crucial position to advise on whether safe care can be given with the staff resources available. How she does this seems to vary considerably from unit to unit. The effect she has on numbers of admissions and closure of beds seems to depend to some extent on how forcefully she presents the facts and an awareness that the underlying philosophy of 'having to cope' is unacceptable. As Rogers and Salvage (1988) point out, 'senior nurses, themselves under stress, often try to contain the distress by forcing nurses to "cope", rather than by taking more decisive collective action to bring the problem to the attention of the employers and the Government'.

How many nurses?

In spite of approximately one third of the hospital budget being spent on nursing salaries, a continuing and major problem for nurse managers is the assessment of how many nurses are actually required. The difficulty becomes even more pronounced when attempting to break this down to skill-mix and clinical gradings. In spite of the importance of this task and the number of research studies done in this area, the tools available have often been poorly designed or misused and the findings have varied considerably from one institution to another. The complexity and variety of nursing continues to thwart the nurse manager in reaching a decision on establishment figures, but from the legal point of view these are a central concern in any accusation of poor care due to inadequate staffing.

Most methods of forecasting nurse numbers required have focused on systems that measure workload related to dependency of the patients being nursed (Senior 1979). Patients are divided into categories, usually between three and nine distinctive groups being identified. For example, in a five-category range, category one would be totally helpless patients and category five, fully ambulant patients. More refined methods such as 'Monitor' and 'Criteria for Care' include an analysis of nursing activity including time spent on meal-breaks, catering and domestic duties as well as direct nursing care. Quality assessment can also be built into a system and with the use of computer programs the complexities of predicting 'how many nurses' may begin to produce some more reliable answers (Senior 1988). Most work has been done in the general area, but systems for other fields are being developed. The calculation of community nurse numbers is the one requiring most attention as several factors have changed the workloads in this area. Most notably these are early discharge, keeping patients in the community rather than hospitalising them and a growing requirement for learner nurses to spend time accompanying the community nurses about their work. The community nurse manager is becoming increasingly aware that it is as important for her to inform medical colleagues of the potential dangers of increasing workloads as it is for her hospital counterpart.

The potential negligence of the nurse manager who gets her sums wrong is only recently being acknowledged. In the past, the blame for a failure to give safe care was always placed firmly on the clinical nurse. However, although no cases have yet been through the civil courts, managers have been criticised in the context of the professional conduct committee of the United Kingdom Central Council for a failure to respond to inadequate staffing levels.

Skill-mix

Skill-mix of nursing staff is also a factor relating to patient safety. There is no doubt that following the increased throughput and shorter length of hospital stay of patients there is a need for a higher proportion of skilled nurses in both hospital and community. It is particularly noticeable in the psychiatric area where large mental illness and mental handicap hospitals have closed with many patients discharged into community care still requiring a high level of support.

Traditionally, the National Health Service has abused the unqualified and second-level nurse. In spite of the potential dangers of negligent care being given to patients in these circumstances (see Chapter 4), managers still persist in continuing to use staff inappropriately due to shortages or for financial reasons. The appearance of the support worker in conjunction with the implementation of Project 2000 is a recent area of debate. The assumption that supervision will negate any adverse effects does not necessarily stand up in law (see p. 38) and both inexperienced worker and delegating nurse can be found negligent if harm results to the patient.

The enrolled nurse's position has been particularly difficult. Her role has varied from being treated as less responsible than a third-year student nurse to being in charge of a ward. Convenience seems to have been the only criterion for this variation. Again, it is usually the enrolled nurse herself who has had to take the blame for negligent care even when the circumstance has been the abuse of her position by expecting her to perform as a registered nurse. Section 18(2) of the Nurses Rules 1983 states clearly that she is required to develop competences to assist in carrying out certain functions under the direction of a registered nurse. She may also accept delegated nursing tasks and in these circumstances she must also be able to refuse if she does not have the necessary knowledge and skills (see p. 57). In a unit under pressure through lack of registered nurses, the enrolled nurse may not feel that she has much choice, but in law she must assert herself and thereby safeguard her patients.

The clinical grading structure (DHSS 1988) does provide for some enrolled nurses legitimately to be given further responsibility. A post-holder at Scale D 'is expected to carry out all forms of care without direct supervision and may be required to demonstrate procedures to and supervise qualified and/or unqualified staff'. A requirement for this post can be first-level registration or 'second-level registration plus a recognised post-basic certificate, or to have an equivalent level of skill acquired through experience'. In deciding to employ an enrolled nurse under these contractual arrangements, the nurse manager must assure herself that the enrolled nurse has the necessary skill as it is extending the nurse's role beyond the competences laid down in the Nurses Rules.

The nurse's role may also be extended in the administration of medicines. As was pointed out (p. 74), the law has little interest in laying detailed rules on nurses regarding the administration of medicines. The UKCC in its booklet, *Standard for the Administration of Medicines* (1992), reinforces the professional stance of Clause 4 of the Code and states:

> There is a wide spectrum of situations in which medicines are administered, ranging at one extreme, from the patient in an intensive therapy unit who is totally dependent on registered professional staff for her or his care, at the other extreme, the person in her or his own home administering her or his own medicines . . . The answer to the question of who can administer a medicine must largely depend on where within that spectrum the recipient of the medicines lies . . .

> In the majority of circumstances, a first level registered nurse, a midwife or a second level nurse, each of whom has demonstrated the necessary knowledge and competence, should be able to administer medicines without involving a second person.

The importance of the nurse manager following the guidelines suggested on p. 58 regarding the delegation of responsibilities must be emphasised. The risk of negligence by the nurse, the delegating manager and the employer by vicarious liability will thus be reduced.

Individual differences

A staff nurse working on a surgical ward set herself extremely high standards and the result was that patients allocated to her received excellent and thorough care. However, the ward became extremely busy on two days of the week when surgeons were operating both morning and afternoon. The nurse found this pace difficult to adjust to and would continue to work at her usual steady and rather slow rate. As a result she would complete only part of her workload, her colleagues having to cover for her. The ward sister spoke to her about this on numerous occasions and tried to help her to adjust, without success. Eventually the disciplinary process was initiated against her. When the nurse was on duty one evening after an exceptionally full list, several crises occurred, putting all the nursing staff at full stretch. The nursing officer was informed but did not send any more staff to the ward. The staff nurse in question failed to carry out some vital post-operative observations and as a result a serious deterioration in a patient's condition was missed. It was only because of prompt intervention by the other nurses and doctors that the patient did not die.

Although the nurse in this example was potentially negligent, the nursing officer was also responsible. Although she may have considered that there were sufficient nurses to give safe care, even on such a busy evening, the issue of numbers is only part of the equation. Where one nurse is known to be unable to function effectively in certain situations, management must take account of this. Considering that the nurse was already subject to disciplinary action, there was no question that the difficulty was unrecognised. The same rules regarding delegation to the inexperienced must also apply to the incompetent and however frustrating it may be to the nurse manager when the nurse in question is a registered nurse, the safety of the patients once again must be of paramount importance. It is also important that, if the situation cannot be resolved informally, formal steps are taken in case the only final outcome is dismissal. From the professional and personal point of view it would be preferable to make better use of individual strengths, perhaps by a change of job, rather than having to be aware of the legal perspective which emphasises an individual's weaknesses.

A common solution to staffing shortages is the employment of agency staff. It is impossible for the manager to know the strengths and weaknesses of these individual nurses and therefore a manager could not be held to blame for any of their shortcomings in the same way. There would be no need to knowingly continue to take on an agency nurse identified as being incompetent. However, the legal position of the health authority towards an agency nurse's negligence is debatable. Although the contractual arrangement between the two is different from that between employer and employee, it may well be that the health authority would have to accept some vicarious liability for her actions (see p. 38).

The hours of work

Nurses are contracted to work a set number of hours. Legally there are a number of manpower issues here. Due to the pressure of work, nurses may frequently find themselves working an additional 15–30 minutes per shift in order to finish their work, particularly the documentation. This does not count as overtime but may add up considerably if it occurs frequently. Nurses often feel under pressure to continue with this pattern which becomes the norm for a ward. Although the nurse manager should give back time owing, it is not always seen as acceptable to the nurse to ask for it. If nurses decided not to work beyond their contracted hours it is interesting to speculate on how many beds may have to be closed as a result!

Emotions also run high on the subject of shift work. The adjustment of shift patterns is a frequent exercise in health authorities in an attempt to make for more balanced staffing levels. There is little legislation in this area, although the Factories Act 1961 states that an individual should not work for more than four and a half hours without a thirty-minute break.

Maintaining standards

Clause 11 of the Code requires the nurse to report 'any circumstances which could jeopardise standards of practice'. The definition of what are appropriate standards, whether legally or professionally, is difficult. The law on negligence sets some ground rules (p. 29) but even these require the use of professional judgement. The importance of standards is recognised in the NHS and

Community Care Act 1990. As well as financial audit, the audit of a number of indicators of good care are now being required. Under the Patient's Charter, the patient or client can expect to see the NHS aiming to:

— respect privacy, dignity and religious and cultural beliefs;
— arrange to ensure that everyone, including people with special needs, can use services;
— give information to relatives and friends;
— apply a maximum waiting time for an ambulance service;
— ensure immediate assessment in accident and emergency departments;
— give specific outpatient clinic appointment times and see a patient within 30 minutes of that time;
— minimise the cancellation of operations;
— provide a named nurse;
— agree arrangements for support prior to discharge from hospital.

As pointed out in Chapter 5, these standards are not statutory but information about performance has to be published annually. Publicity is usually a spur towards achievement. For the nurse, many of these standards are not specifically related to nursing care. The development of nursing standards along with nursing audit is making progress, but again has no statutory base. Local contractual arrangements between provider units and commissioners may require the existence and monitoring of standards of care, and any such written statements will provide a pressure on nurse managers in relation to their units.

Clinical nurse responsibility

Considerable anxiety has been expressed by practising nurses regarding the maintenance of standards in the current financial climate (Rowden 1990). With reductions in staffing levels and possible 'dilution' of qualified nurses following skill-mix exercises, such anxiety may be justified. However, the law's concern is with safety, not excellence, and this should be borne in mind by the nurse when expressing any concerns. In spite of the difficulties, there are several reasons why the clinical nurse should take action if she suspects staffing resources are inadequate to maintain safe care. First, unless the nurse manager is given this information, she cannot take the appropriate steps to safeguard patient care. Secondly, a nurse involved in a negligent act as a result of staff shortages must ensure that she has taken reasonable measures to remedy the situation.

A thirty-bed medical ward consisted of six single rooms and a number of small bays. The nurse on duty one night assisted by a student and auxiliary nurse was concerned about their ability to guarantee safety to the very ill and dependent patients in their care. She expressed her concern to the night sister who told her that they would have to cope as she could not let them have another nurse. Wisely, the nurse made a written note of what had been said so that if a patient had suffered as a result, any negligence would have been the night sister's and not the ward staff's.

This response by the nurse to inadequate staffing is legally sound in the short term. If there is no attempt by the nurse manager to remedy the situation when the staffing difficulties continue over a period of time, other avenues must be explored. Employment legislation gives nurses certain rights regarding their conditions of employment. Most health authorities now have a grievance policy, but even without one the employee can still express her concerns to senior management. The nurse's immediate manager should always be given an initial chance to respond and remedy the situation before a formal grievance is made to a more senior level. Grievances should be put in writing and management has a duty to respond. The involvement of the nurse's union representative can often help to support the nurse who may fear victimisation as a result of her stand.

The case of Graham Pink, who complained about staffing levels and subsequently lost his job, has exacerbated this fear (Turner 1992). The introduction of 'gagging clauses' in some contracts of employment has also angered nurses, although being seen as reasonable safeguards for ensuring confidentiality by managers (Carlisle 1992). An example of such a clause is:

> In the course of your normal work, you will come into the possession of confidential information concerning patients and staff. Such information must always be treated as strictly confidential and must not be divulged to any individual organisation, including the press, without prior written approval of the chief executive.

The Code puts a responsibility on the nurse to report concerns to 'an appropriate person or authority'. It is suggested that the route taken is that put forward above and that 'appropriate' people within the organisation are given the chance to respond prior to making decision on when to move beyond these and to whom to turn for further action and support. The Health and Safety at Work Act has such a wide remit that it could be used to protect both staff and patients from inadequate staffing levels. However, it has never been applied in this area, although training staff in how to prioritise care, cope with stress and be assertive would all be potentially useful.

Conclusion

Reporting circumstances that could jeopardise standards or safety has always carried the risk to the individual of being labelled a 'troublemaker' and disloyal to her employer. However, the law's emphasis on the right of the patient to expect safe care of a reasonable standard as stated through the law on negligence provides a useful bridge across from the nurse's professional desire to promote good standards and her fear of the consequence of 'whistleblowing'. What is very apparent from this chapter is that the law requires both the nurse manager and the clinical nurse to perform their roles in an active rather than a passive way. The nurse who fails to point out unsafe practices and the manager who does not argue the repercussions of staffing levels and skill-mix on patient safety are both professionally incompetent and potentially negligent.

In *Bull and Another* v. *Devon AHA* 1989, although it was accepted that there was no individual negligence, it was established that the system in which the service was operating was so 'precarious' and 'operating on such a knife edge' that the hospital had failed to plan for the foreseeable requirements of the patient. The hospital was found to be in breach of its duty and compensation was paid to a baby for brain damage at birth caused by what should have been avoidable delays in the attendance of the necessary staff. This example should again demonstrate the importance of staff bringing situations of potential risk to the attention of management.

References

Beckett A and Young A P 1989. *Health and Safety at Work. Part II Checks and Balances.* Diploma in Nursing, Distance Learning Centre, South Bank Polytechnic, London.
Brazier M 1987. *Medicine, Patients and the Law.* Penguin Books, Harmondsworth, Middlesex.

Carlisle D 1992. A Clause for Alarm? *Nursing Times* **88** (24) 29–30.

Department of Health and Social Security 1988. *New Clinical Grading Structure for Nurses, Midwives and Health Visitiors*, EL(88)P33. DHSS, London.

Department of Health 1990. *The NHS and Community Care Act 1990; Removal of Crown Immunities*. HMSO, London.

Department of Health 1991. *The Patient's Charter*. HMSO, London.

Rogers R and Salvage J 1988. *Nurses at Risk. A Guide to Health and Safety at Work*. Heinemann, Oxford.

Rowden R 1990. Quality of care. *Nursing Times* **86** (8), 21 Feb, pp. 29–30.

Senior O E 1979. *Dependency and Establishments*. Royal College of Nursing, London.

Senior O E 1988. Manpower planning objectives and information systems. In Hudson D (ed.), *Recent Advances in Nursing: Nursing Administration*. Churchill Livingstone, London.

Statutory Instruments 1983. *The Nurses, Midwives and Health Visitors Rules*. Approval, Order No. 873. HMSO, London.

Turner T 1992. The Indomitable Mr. Pink. *Nursing Times* **88** (24), 10 June, pp. 26–28.

United Kingdom Central Council 1992. *Code of Professional Conduct*, 3rd edition. UKCC, London.

United Kingdom Central Council 1992. *Standards for the Administration of Medicines*. UKCC, London.

CHAPTER 10

Health and Safety at Work

*Report to an appropriate person or authority where it appears that the
health or safety of colleagues is at risk, as such circumstances may
compromise standards of practice and care.*

How safe is work? Can nursing damage your health? One indicator
of health and safety at work comes from accident statistics. Staff
may be injured during the course of their duties and nurses are
particularly at risk. Many injuries occur in Accident and Emergency Departments but other high-risk areas are operating theatres
and hospital grounds. All adult wards tend to have marked accident statistics while the safest wards for staff are probably those
for children. In addition, a number of accidents take place in
people's homes.

The nature of the accidents reported must also be of concern. For
one health authority, the largest number of staff accidents involved
needlestick and associated 'sharps' injuries with the ever-present
risk of infection to the nurses involved. Assault by patients was
the second highest category, followed by falls, injuries involving
equipment and back injuries while moving patients (see Table
10.1).
Other statistics – for example, figures on nurse sickness levels and
drug errors – all help to build a picture of the workplace.

Such information is vital to both nurse and manager in focusing
where and what resources are most needed. This chapter will
explore the legal framework influencing the use of these resources
in maintaining health and safety of colleagues.

Type: Location	Assaults	Back and other injury handling patients	Falls	Injured by equipment	Needle-stick and sharps injuries	Total
General wards (18)	8	24	4	8	50	94
Psychiatric wards (11)	48	1	3	3	1	56
Geriatric wards (8)	8	12	2	9	8	39
Paediatric wards (5)	3	1	3	1	2	10
Midwifery unit	—	—	—	—	3	3
Accident and Emergency Dpt.	7	—	—	7	21	35
Operating theatres	—	—	3	4	20	27
Hospital grounds	3	—	11	9	5	28
Community – patient's home	3	4	1	—	3	11
Total	80	42	27	41	113	

Table 10.1 Accidents to nurses by location and type (adapted from accident statistics for one HA)

Safety at work – the legal base

A number of statutes have a strong influence on the safety of the working environment (Beckett and Young 1989). The most important of these is the Health and Safety at Work etc. Act 1974. Previous Acts had tended to concentrate on specific groups of workers, but this Act applies to all except those in domestic employment and is wide-ranging in its powers. Because of the cost of implementing this legislation, a drawback to the nurse has been the rather minimal interpretation of its requirements. Many of these only lay a duty on the employer to act 'as is reasonably practicable' rather than laying down an absolute duty. However, it remains the most important legislation in this area in recent years, particularly since the lifting of Crown immunity (p. 122). Health authorities can be prosecuted for a failure to implement the Health and Safety at Work Act.

In addition, particular duties are laid on employers in the hospital or clinic setting towards visitors. People should have protection from injury as a result of defects of the property and the Occupiers' Liability Acts 1957 and 1984 have done much to clarify the anomalies previously existing under civil law (Eddey 1987). The redress for the injured visitor, whether he be worker, patient, relative or trespasser, will be a claim for compensation (see p. 139).

The law of torts still remains of major importance to both the nurse and the patient in receiving some personal redress for either negligence or trespass in the form of assault and battery. The outcome of legal cases against a health authority often leads to a review of practices with subsequent improvement of the work situation. However, both nurse and patient are often reluctant to take such legal action. The patient who has suffered harm often finds it too distressing to face the long-drawn-out legal processes that ensue from the taking of such action. The nurse may feel a sense of loyalty to her employer or colleagues that make her unwilling to sue them for negligence. When assaulted by a patient, she may find it morally difficult to proceed against someone who has been in her care although having the legal right to do so (see p. 152).

As was pointed out on page 27, the individual has no legal redress in negligence if no harm resulted or consequential harm cannot be proved. The patient, or the nurse on his behalf if he is unable to act for himself, can take some action in this situation. The Hospital Complaints Procedure Act 1985 ensures that any complaints made about the way a patient has been treated must be investigated (see p. 70). In addition, the nurse disturbed by some defect of her working environment can bring this to the attention of her health and safety representative (p. 140) or use her local grievance procedure (see p. 132).

The Health and Safety at Work Act

The overall objective of this Act is:

> To secure the health, safety and welfare of persons at work and protecting persons other than persons at work against risks to health and safety arising out of, or in connection with, the activities of persons at work. (Section 1)

An interpretation of this rather long-winded statement seems to indicate that the Act also has patients in mind as receivers of the work that nurses carry out as well as employees themselves. The Act proceeded to lay down the general duties of employers and employees and although these show some resemblance to the duty of care as developed by the law on negligence, the great strength of this legislation is the aim of preventing damage rather than waiting for damage to occur before any legal action is possible.

The employer's overall duty is to ensure the health, safety and welfare of his employees (Howells and Barrett 1982). He only has to take reasonable steps to ensure this. For example, where there is a high risk of some practice causing damage, then it must be reasonable to take steps to reduce the potential for harm. On the other hand, where there is only a small risk, then less stringent action would be expected from the employer. The law also accepts that there are some risks that it is scientifically extremely difficult to reduce and the Act does not expect the employer to achieve the impossible. The employer's duties can be laid out as follows.

Plant and equipment must be provided and maintained. Heating and ventilation systems are important for the health of both patients and nurses. A poorly maintained heating plant will often malfunction at the first cold spell of autumn. Portable heaters used in such an emergency create additional fire hazards; while patients swathed in blankets are unable to move about or freely carry out many of the other activities of living. Proper ventilation systems in the operating theatres are important in controlling infection as well as making for more acceptable working conditions for the surgeons and nurses. The provision of equipment is vital for many nursing activities. This must be suitable for what is required of it and for the environment in which it is to be used. The seemingly simple bed is a good example of the number of features that must be present to meet the needs of both the patient and the nurse. The equipment must also be reliable. It is of no use to the nurse if for 50 per cent of the time a hoist is out of action. The employer therefore also has a duty to provide sufficient personnel to detect and repair any equipment faults.

Premises must be maintained to a safe level. This is a particular problem in the National Health Service where many of the buildings used are old and since the inception of the Health Service in 1948, have never had sufficient money spent on their fabric. The safety of hospital grounds also needs consideration. As was shown in the accident statistics, this is a high-risk area, particularly for falls. Adequate lighting both in and out of buildings is important and steps must be kept safe. Clear signposting will assist both staff, patients and visitors to keep to well-maintained areas. However, under the Occupiers' Liability Act 1984, the health authority also has a duty to provide safe premises to trespassers although the nature of this duty is less than to legitimate visitors. Thus hazards in rarely used areas need to be marked as well as those in more populated parts of the hospital or clinic. Floor washing is a common example of an occasion when it is important to have clearly displayed notices saying 'Beware, wet floor' and hazard signs. A patient or visitor slipping on a wet floor where there were no such notices would have grounds for claiming compensation under the Occupiers' Liability Act 1957. In addition, the employer needs to be aware of this failure to maintain safe premises under the Health and Safety at Work Act.

Another overall employer responsibility under the Act is the provision of a safe working environment as far as is reasonably practicable. This gives an extremely broad remit and therefore potentially empowers the employer to make a detailed response to the many facets affecting the safety of staff. As has already been stated, the response in practice tends to be somewhat minimal in the National Health Service. Physical safety is more likely to be addressed than mental stress; and of the physical risks, it is often only the most obvious that seem to merit action (Rogers and Salvage 1988).

The issue of giving information and training to staff is a recurrent theme of the Health and Safety at Work Act. Employees must be informed of specific hazards. Sometimes this creates a potential conflict as the employer may be unwilling to create unnecessary alarm, for example of an outbreak of Legionnaire's disease. The health authority has a particular responsibility in relation to hazardous substances, for example gases and radioactive materials. The Control of Substances Hazardous to Health Regulations 1989 place additional responsibilities on the employer to those under the Health and Safety at Work Act. It is rarely adequate to give information only. In a large number of situations this must be supplemented by training, for example in the area of handling equipment or patients. This is such an important area both legally and professionally that it is dealt with as a separate issue (see p. 143).

The employer has a duty to provide periodic medical examinations for those nurses exposed to particular risks. Many would agree that all nurses are in a stressful and hazardous job and should therefore be given this facility. However, as in other areas, the implementation of this part of the Act again tends to be somewhat minimal. Those caring for patients undergoing radiation therapy are checked, but only if they are working in that area on a long-term basis rather than over a period of only a few months. If nurses are in contact with a patient with open tuberculosis, then all of them are tested. Otherwise, medical examination tends to be limited to the start of employment.

The Act also lays a duty on the employer to consult with trade unions, usually through safety committees which will include appointed safety representatives. For the employee, the local safety representative is extremely important in ensuring that health and safety needs are recognised and that action is taken by the employer. This person, appointed by the appropriate union or professional body, is often seen to be more approachable by the nurse than is the manager. In addition, the representative will have the knowledge to recognise the strength of the nurse's criticisms and the skill to present the complaint to management. In some organisations, there has been a number of difficulties in the appointment of safety representatives. Employers have made it hard for representatives to take paid time off to undertake the training required and further time away from their normal employment in order to carry out their functions of advising workers and attending the appropriate meetings. In addition, relevant information has not always been available, for example on accidents or hazards in the workplace.

A final duty of the employer is the provision of personal safety items free of charge. Thus uniform is provided free, as this is, in effect, protective clothing, and personal alarms are given to community nurses to help safeguard them from attack when visiting patients in their own homes.

The employee has two important and complementary duties under the Act. These are:

1. to take reasonable care for the health and safety of himself and of other persons who may be affected by his acts or omissions at work;
2. to cooperate with other persons to enable the carrying out of the statutory duties imposed by the Health and Safety at Work Act.

The first point again clearly has its roots in the tort of negligence. In fact, the nurse failing to take such reasonable care can be sued by a fellow employee who suffers harm as a result (see p. 58). In addition, under the Act a nurse could be prosecuted for any such acts or omissions. The second point underlines the two-way process envisaged by the Act in implementing health and safety practice in the workplace.

The manager can play the role of either employer or employee. With the devolvement of management responsibility to smaller units, the nurse manager may find herself playing both roles. She has the needs of any employee as regards a safe system of working and adequate information and training. On the other hand, she must monitor those indicators of a safe environment mentioned at the start of this chapter, recognise and set up such training as is needed by the nurses working in her unit and ensure proper consultation channels exist.

In order to implement the Act, two bodies were set up. The Health and Safety Commission consists of representatives of employers, employees, local authorities and professional bodies. Its activities include the making of regulations and codes of practice. Regulations are legally binding and must be approved by the Secretary of State. Codes of practice are issued for guidance. The Commission also provides an information and advisory service, supports research and publishes research findings. Finally, if necessary, it will investigate accidents or other occurrences

The Health and Safety Executive is the operating arm of the Commission and has the power to enforce the statutory provisions of the Act by means of the Inspectorate. An inspector has wide-ranging powers which include power of entry, power to investigate by the taking of samples and photographs, seizing substances causing imminent danger, ordering premises to be left undisturbed, requiring persons to give information and requiring access to documents. It is the inspector who instigates a prosecution under the Act, not an employer or employee and he can also serve an improvement notice or a prohibition order. In theory this seems adequate authority to improve the safety of the workplace. In practice, the number of inspectors has declined with an ever-increasing workload and the fines following successful prosecution are not always high enough to act as a deterrent. A nurse unable to get a satisfactory response to a safety hazard from her manager can always contact the local inspector, usually via her safety representative.

The influence of Europe

Law initiated in the European Community as a result of the Treaty of Rome has had an influence on health and safety at work in member countries. The development and publication of directives lay a legal duty on community members to implement their content through their own legislation. In the UK, this results in the making of regulations (as described above). It seems likely that if these fall short of the requirements of the directive, the courts must interpret the law in line with the meaning of the directive.

Of general relevance are the Health and Safety (General Provisions) Regulations 1992, and the Workplace (Health and Safety and Welfare) Regulations 1992. These aim to improve health and safety management and set out some general requirements relating to the working environment, safety, facilities and housekeeping. Other directives have led to more specific regulations relating to the provision and use of equipment, manual handling and visual display units. Although under the Maastricht Treaty the UK has withdrawn from implementing the Social Charter, it has maintained its commitment to health and safety at work. There is no doubt that from January 1993, the Single European Act 1987 is having a major impact on the UK workplace.

Information and training

The employer has a statutory duty to keep employees informed on topics that are likely to affect health and safety. This will include information on particular diseases that have health implications to the nurse (e.g. AIDS) as well as treatments that carry risks to those administering them (e.g. the toxic effects of certain drugs). How well this is done tends to vary considerably from one health authority to another and the safety representatives do find that the onus is sometimes placed on them to ask for relevant information. Safety representatives also find that information on accident statistics, health and safety checks by inspectors and frequency of other environmental monitoring is not necessarily volunteered without a formal request.

Policy statements on safety matters are seen as an important part of the Act in informing employees and assisting them to maintain safe practices. They should include:

- procedures for reporting hazards to management;
- procedures for reporting accidents and keeping records of accidents;
- procedures for keeping staff informed of known dangers and necessary precautions;
- systems for identifying training needs and ensuring that training is carried out.

A particular value of a policy is that it is enforceable through disciplinary procedures. However, against this advantage must be set several disadvantages. Policy-making must involve consultation of interested parties, thus allowing all points of view to be expressed, but this can be extremely time-consuming. Safety policies may take several years before finally agreed, which is scarcely helpful to nurses awaiting guidance. Once formulated, a policy then tends to stay operational for a number of years though it may become out of date and inappropriate as circumstances change. The long-winded procedures also tend to deter the employer from producing safety policies for any but those situations that have very serious implications on patient or staff safety, for example drug administration and lifting.

It is therefore not unusual to find another format being used by the employer for transmitting information on health and safety. Written guidelines on nursing procedures and practices are usually developed by a small group of nurses with particular skills and experience. An advantage of this approach is the opportunity it provides for easier and quicker updating as knowledge (especially research-based knowledge) and equipment change. However, consultation is limited and there is therefore a danger that some of those with particular expertise in the subject or in the training skills necessary for implementation may be omitted from the process. Secondly, information written for guidance cannot be enforced by law.

The commitment to training is vital legally for both the employer and employee. Quite apart from being a key part of the Health and Safety at Work Act, the giving of proper training in a number of areas will protect the employer from being sued for negligence by an employee who suffers harm at work as a result of inadequate knowledge and skill. Protection against harm is as important to the employee and training will hopefully help to provide the nurse with the ability to avoid dangers or limit their effects, for example, when caring for patients with certain infections.

Training will need to be given to qualified and unqualified nurses alike. Support workers who are involved with handling and lifting patients need as effective a training in this area as the student nurse who will proceed to registration. The health authority has a duty to safeguard both employee and patient. The argument that some members of staff will always be working under the supervision of others is unlikely to hold up in court when it is a common and clearly defined area of health and safety. Student nurse training will include a marked amount of training and supervision in health and safety matters. Lifting, the administration of drugs by injection, the management of intravenous therapy, the control of infection and the handling of aggression and violence are areas of particular concern.

Sufficient training must be given prior to a student working full-time in the clinical area to ensure her own safety and that of others, both patients and staff. However, the college of nursing has a responsibility to include ongoing training and practice throughout the training programme in order to enable student nurses to become confident and capable of dealing with different situations with decreasing levels of supervision.

The qualified nurse also requires training in a number of areas and, if appropriate, practice under supervision of what is learnt. Even for something that should have received adequate attention either in training or in a previous post, the employer would be unwise to assume that this training was sufficient. For new members of staff it is usually acknowledged as good practice to arrange for refresher courses. Ongoing training is especially important where the knowledge base of nursing practice is continually being extended. This will apply in a number of instances, for example, in relation to certain infections where the knowledge of how the disease is transmitted becomes more refined and in the handling and moving of patients where new techniques and equipment are continually being developed. It is not sufficient for the employer to put on these refresher and updating courses. The nurse manager for each unit must encourage her staff to attend by providing the necessary extra nurses to cover for their absence while on these courses. Nurses working in specialist areas will often face particular risks not shared across all units. For example, the community nurse will need specialist training to enable her to lift safely in the patient's home and the nurse in the psychiatric area may need a greater input on preventing and dealing safely with violence.

Careful record-keeping of any training is important under the Health and Safety at Work Act and in case of later legal action for negligence. The records should be sufficiently detailed to make clear what was taught rather than just the overall area of instruction. It is also useful to include the name of the instructor as well as the date(s) on which the training took place.

Documentation of accidents and incidents

There is a legal requirement on employers to report accidents and dangerous occurrences under the Reporting of Injuries, Diseases and Dangerous Occurrences Regulations 1985. All injuries resulting from accidents at work that cause incapacity for more than four days must be reported directly to the Health and Safety Executive and there are rules governing the reporting of certain diseases. However, there is still a large number of incidents of ill health among nurses, which are probably occupation-related but do not have to be reported. This also makes the accident statistics produced (see Table 10.1 page 136) rather incomplete unless other information is also noted.

It is important that a nurse involved in an accident or dangerous

	Surname
	First Name(s)
	Address
STATEMENT OF ACCIDENT TO	
EMPLOYEE	Married/Single
	National Insurance No.

This report is CONFIDENTIAL and must be completed immediately the accident has occurred.
All details must be completed and the form sent to the Sector Administration office.

Ward/Dept. .... Job Title ....

Date Employment commenced ....

Was the injured employee directly employed by the District? ....

Date and time of accident ....

Was the accident reported to you at the time it occurred? ....

If not, when was it reported to you? ....

What hours would employee normally have worked on the date of the accident? ....

....

What hours were actually worked? ....

Did employee remain on duty after the accident? ....

If not. date and time ceased work ....

Was employee seen by a doctor? ....

If yes, please specify: Casualty Officer/Own G.P./Other ....

Is employee at home or in hospital? ....

If in hospital please specify ....

State circumstances of accident: in particular state whether employee was engaged in the duties attached to his/her post

....

....

....

....

....

....

....

Exact nature of injury (eg left or right limb) ....

Description of equipment involved ....

....

Has it been retained for inspection? .... Where?.....................................

Were any other parties involved in the accident? ....

....

Particulars of any witnesses:—

Name .... Name ....

Address .... Address ....

....

Tel. No. .... Tel. No. ....

Signature of member of staff in charge at time of accident:

....

GH 740

Figure 10.1 Sample staff accident form

incident fills in the appropriate form (see Figures 10.1 and 10.2). First, proper care must be taken of the nurse involved in the incident, for example, by follow-up action in the Accident and Emergency Department or the Occupational Health Department. Secondly, the collating and publication of accident figures should affect future policies and training requirements. Thirdly, if there is the possibility of a legal action for negligence, it is likely to be many years before this comes to court (see p. 33) and precise details of what happened and other facts relevant to the situation must be carefully recorded. From the legal point of view, too much detail is always preferable to too little. The police may become involved, for example, if a nurse has been assaulted by a patient; careful records will assist them in dealing with the incident (see p. 151). Finally, if there is the possibility of the nurse claiming compensation for injury either through industrial injury benefits or the Criminal Injuries Compensation Board, records will assist with the processing of these claims.

Lifting and handling patients

Back pain is a major occupational hazard for nurses and the legislation controlling lifting and handling of patients has been patchy and difficult to implement.

A quotation from *The Guide to the Handling of Patients* (National Back Pain Association 1992) sums up the problem:

> The adult human form is an awkward burden to lift or carry. Weighing up to 100 kg. or more, it has no handles, it is not rigid and it is liable to severe damage if mishandled or dropped. In bed, a patient is placed inconveniently for lifting, and the placing of a load in such a situation would be tolerated by few industrial workers.

Therefore, lifting and moving patients involves a large number of factors. The organisation of the whole environment is vital for safety as well as the mechanics of lifting. Clothing, footwear, amount of space, provision of suitable equipment, sufficient staff and proper training are all important. A major problem is the fact that a patient is not a static object! Patients vary in the degree of cooperation they can give and even a helpful patient may suddenly become frightened while being lifted and jeopardise the safety of both himself and the nurses by unexpected actions.

Legally, there have been a number of recent developments from

Ward/Clinic		Consul

REPORT ON VIOLENT INCIDENT

Surname		Unit
First Name		
Date of Birth		
Address		Se

This report is CONFIDENTIAL

1. It is intended to ensure that violent incidents are notified with the least possible delay.

2. It is NOT intended to replace the present STATEMENT OF INCIDENT TO PATIENTS OR VISITORS form, which will also be required, and should be routed as at present.

A quarterly summary of violent incidents will be given to the Medical Committee Executive.

Affix documentation label to, or complete manually, data box above. In addition complete status details as follows:

Inpatient   Day Patient   Out Patient (current)

Out Patient (old)   Informal   Formal

The following should be completed for all incidents:

Hospital   Ward/Dept

Room/area   Consultant

Date of Incident   Time of Incident

Name of Person Making Report   Status

Was violence threatened?   Inflicted

Was damage/injury done (or threatened) to (yes or tick where appropriate)

Property   Nurses   Doctors

Other staff (specify)   Others (specify)

Was Statement of Accident (or Incident) completed   **Was weapon used (specify)**

How much warning of violence was given

Were drugs a factor in the incident

Was the patient under the influence of alcohol

Was there a history of violence

Was this history known to those involved

Was help called from: other staff on the ward/dept.

Nursing Officer/Night Sister   Staff on other wards

Patients Doctor/Duty Doctor   Police/Fire Brigade

Others (specify)

Was medication given   With consent   Without consent

Was physical restraint necessary   How many staff/helpers were there

Was the incident satisfactorily resolved

Was the patient transferred/discharged (specify)

Date of staff discussion

WVA 880

Figure 10.2 Sample violent incident form

the somewhat limited nature of the Health and Safety at Work Act with its emphasis on what is 'reasonably practicable'. The new regulations arising from EC directives seem to impose a higher duty on employers, nearer to that of 'practicability'. In addition, the Manual Handling Operations Regulations put a greater emphasis on the provision and use of equipment in order to avoid manual handling and, where manual handling is unavoidable, the necessity of assessment of both the load and the environment. Two possible assessment tools are shown in Figure 10.3. In addition, these regulations propose that a maximum load for lifting by one person is 25 kg, therefore for two people, 50 kg. Any patient weighing 50 kg or more must be deemed as heavy and alternatives to manual lifting considered. However, these figures are only guidelines and no legislation can cover the urgent or emergency situation where circumstances are far from ideal.

In spite of precautions, there seems to be a never-ending stream of nurses who are either off sick for long periods or even have to give up a nursing career owing to damaged backs. A number of these nurses take their employer to court for negligence regarding the provision of a safe working environment. The courts are responding to their predicament and awarding damages. Such case law is also an important influence on employers to consider greater investment in training and equipment.

Infections

Infections are a major source of ill health among nurses and affect the efficiency with which they can carry out their duties as well as increasing the workload on colleagues when they have to go off sick. This in turn puts patients at risk when staffing levels are reduced (see p. 121). Much of this infection cannot be linked specifically to the hospital environment, but the nature of the nurse's work can sap the individual's immune system, making her more prone to many bacteria and viruses. From the patient's viewpoint, a stay in hospital may well be prolonged and recovery delayed by a hospital-acquired infection.

In spite of the importance of this area, there is very little legislation in addition to the general duties imposed by the Health and Safety at Work Act. A nurse's conditions of employment may state that the employee should act responsibly in relation to her health but there seems to be little attempt to provide a more hygienic

Patient Ability Ratings

Grade	Patient's ability
1	Patient is unable to assist in any way. May be unconscious. Should be considered as a 'dead weight'.
2	Patient aware of surroundings. May have ability to assist in a limited way.
3	Patient able to assist to a moderate degree. May however be uncooperative or likely to behave in a random manner.
4	Patient able to assist a little and cooperate with care staff when being moved.
5	Patient needs minimal assistance, though supervision required.
6	Patient able to move on own, unaided. May require minimal supervision.

Environment Rating

Grade	Environment
*** Hazards present. Double check before proceeding. Seek advice if uncertain about your abilities	Difficult environment due to lack of space, patient, machine-equipment interacting hazards related to patient placement. *Examples* (i) Community nursing in patient's home, cramped, loose carpets, etc. (ii) Intensive Care Unit, Theatre, Dialysis Centre, Burns Unit. (iii) Bathroom, restricted toilet area, getting into and out of car.
** Check carefully before proceeding	Reasonable environment but some difficulty could be encountered. *Example* (i) Orthopaedic ward where patients may be on traction. (ii) Geriatric or children's ward with cot sides on beds. (iii) Unit using water beds.
* Take normal routine precautions	Functional and well designed environment. *Example* Modern, spacious, well-lit ward.

Figure 10.3 Assessment of situation prior to lifting (Health and Safety Commission 1988)

environment. For example, handwashing, a prime method of reducing cross-infection, is not encouraged by having only two washbasins for the nurses in a thirty-bed ward.

Failure by the employer to take reasonable measures can, as already mentioned, lead to an action for negligence and this can bring some pressure to bear to take more positive steps in some circumstances. Proper training in infection control is now being seen as important due to the increase of patients with HIV infections (RCN 1986). Accident statistics that highlight a very high incidence of needlestick or other 'sharps' injuries may well support a move towards a wider availability of hepatitis B vaccination to nurses working in areas other than those conventionally considered to be high-risk.

The situation of the nurse who may be carrying HIV is becoming increasingly debated. At the start of employment, the prospective employer has the right to demand any medical screening considered appropriate within the constraints of discriminatory practices. However, once employment has commenced, the employer must have reasonable grounds for demanding a blood test. If the employee refuses and is then dismissed, it may be quite difficult for the employer to prove that he had acted reasonably unless the employee had been acting in such a way as to recklessly endanger public health (Young 1992). It is worth noting that there have been no known cases of a patient or fellow employee contracting AIDS from a nurse.

In situations of ill health, for whatever cause, the nurse may choose to seek advice from the Occupational Health Department. Although the usual rules of confidentiality apply, occupational health staff are sometimes put in an awkward position regarding disclosure of medical information that has potential implications to patient safety. The employer may suggest that failure to disclose could be potential negligence. Following the guidelines in the UKCC booklet on confidentiality and the public interest (1987) should assist staff in this area.

Violence

Violence, both verbal and physical, is met by nurses in many settings (DHSS 1987). It is important that the training offered by the employer covers preventive measures as well as techniques for dealing with the physical manifestations of violence. For example, nurses should be aware that fear and frustration often act as triggers, therefore, giving adequate information and a calm tolerant manner may defuse a potentially violent incident. In addition to training, the health authority has a responsibility to provide a safe environment in high-risk areas by the provision of non-verbal call systems, personal alarms for community nurses and shatterproof glass in areas where the acutely disturbed are to be nursed. It is rarely considered 'reasonable' to expect the employer to provide measures in other areas, although a spate of incidents may bring about further change. For example, a series of assaults in the hospital grounds may initiate more frequent patrols by security staff. However, it is unlikely that a nurse suing her employer for negligence after she suffered serious injury as a result of an assault in a general medical ward would receive any damages via this route.

Legally, the nurse has two other avenues open to her if she is attacked by a patient. First, the police should be informed. Assault and battery is a crime and the police may be able to prosecute. However, for a prosecution to succeed, the patient must have the necessary intention (see p. 2) and if he is mentally ill or under the influence of drugs or alcohol, the police may consider that there is no point in proceeding as any prosecution would be likely to fail, unless injuries were severe. It is still important for the police to be informed in case the nurse later wishes to apply for compensation under the Criminal Injuries Compensation Board.

Assault and battery is also a civil wrong and therefore the nurse has the legal right to sue the patient for damages under the tort of trespass (see p. 109). Several nurses have done so and won their cases although, as explained (p. 137), nurses are often unwilling to take this action. In one case, the patient sued was a long-term patient in a mental hospital whose repeated attacks on the nurses went unremedied by criminal law. As a means of drawing attention to their plight, they successfully sued the patient. The judge criticised the nurses for their action as the patient had no money to pay the damages. In so doing, he clearly failed to understand the frustration that nurses feel in this situation.

Another concern to nurses is how much force can be used to restrain a violent patient. Manual restraint should only be used where it is necessary to protect the patient or others from harm. The amount of force used should only be the minimum required, otherwise the staff themselves could be accused of assault and battery. Occasionally, it is then necessary to use seclusion which involves isolation of the patient in a room. In both situations it is important that the nursing officer and doctor are informed, careful observation of the patient is maintained and a record made of the incident (RCN 1979).

Psychological health

Health and safety at work is more likely to be linked in people's minds with physical than psychological conditions. However, the pressures of the many changes going on in the health care scene at present do have an effect, not just on standards of care and patient safety as pointed out in Chapter 9, but also on the health and safety of the individual nurse (Rogers and Salvage 1988).

Stress is a word that is currently overused; in reality it is unwanted or excessive stress that creates problems. This may lead to physical changes in the body and then to physical illness such as high blood pressure and gastrointestinal upsets, or emotional responses with a loss of concentration and a reduction in ability to communicate effectively. Either way, the result is a less effective nurse who may not be able to care adequately for her patients. Stresses at work may arise from workload, shiftwork, job or role changes, an increase in autonomy and responsibility, a change in the peer group and fear of job loss.

Unfortunately, as psychological health is so rarely planned for, even when appreciated and acknowledged by managers, the law can have little influence in this area. The major spur to action is a wish to improve productivity and effectiveness of staff. For the nurse, the use of Clause 13 of the Code is therefore of importance in attempting to bring the psychological health of colleagues to the attention of management and to use this as a basis for wider ranging discussions on the improvement of staff morale and the provision of adequate support.

Staff sickness

As seen, there are a number of reasons for staff sickness, some of which will be work related. Repeated short-term sickness may be the subject of informal or formal action under a sickness policy and although the stated aim of management is to help the nurse, she may experience this as being very similar to disciplinary action. It is ironic that the stress component of some illness is then exacerbated by such action. The sick nurse has certain statutory rights. The National Health Service has always given better conditions than those required by law (see Table 10.2). Outside the health service, the nurse should be aware that she may receive only the minimum legal requirement statutory sick pay (SSP). This is paid by an employer for the first 20 weeks and thereafter reverts to the responsibility of the DSS.

Professionally, the nurse often experiences a dilemma about going off sick. She tends to feel guilty leaving staff to cover for her and may often stay on duty with an infection even though by doing so she is actually putting the health of her patients and colleagues at risk. In addition, it can be safer for a manager to reorganise workloads in the absence of a member of staff than for the ill nurse to continue working with less than normal efficiency.

First year continuous service	Full pay one month	Half pay one month
Second year continuous service	Full pay two months	Half pay two months
Third year continuous service	Full pay four months	Half pay four months
Fourth, fifth years continuous service	Full pay five months	Half pay five months
After five years continuous service	Full pay six months	Half pay six months

Table 10.2 Whitley Council sickness benefits

Conclusion

The legislation in existence puts responsibility on both employer and employee to consider the health and safety of staff. However, to do this effectively costs a great deal of money and resources and as a result, the implementation of statutory instruments tends to be minimal. Only the threat of civil action seems to galvanise the employer into further action. In some ways such a stance is understandable in the present political climate but it does result in only those safety matters that are urgent and usually involving the physical health of the nurse and patient being addressed.

Legally, those matters affecting the psychological health of nurses have to be dealt with by other means.

References

Beckett A and Young A P 1989. *Health and Safety at Work. Part II: Checks and Balances*. Diploma in Nursing. Distance Learning Centre, South Bank Polytechnic, London.

Department of Health and Social Security 1987. *Report of Conference on Violence to Staff*. HMSO, London.

Eddey K J 1987. *The English Legal System*, 4th edition. Sweet & Maxwell, London.

Howells R and Barret B 1982. *Health and Safety at Work Act: A Guide for Managers*, 2nd edition. Institute of Personnel Management, London.

National Back Pain Association 1992. *The Guide to the Handling of Patients*, 3rd edition. NBPA and RCN, London.

Rogers R and Salvage J 1988. *Nurses at Risk. A Guide to Health and Safety at Work*. Heinemann, London.

Royal College of Nursing 1986. *Nursing Guidelines on the Management of Patients in Hospital and the Community Suffering from AIDS*. RCN, London.

Royal College of Nursing 1979. *Seclusion and Restraint in Hospitals and Units for the Mentally Disordered*. RCN, London.

United Kingdom Central Council 1987. *Confidentiality*, Advisory Paper. UKCC, London.

United Kingdom Central Council 1992. *Code of Professional Conduct*, 3rd edition. UKCC, London.

Young A P 1992. *Case Studies in Law and Nursing*. Chapman and Hall, London.

CHAPTER 11

Teaching and Assessing

Assist professional colleagues, in the context of your own knowledge,
experience and sphere of responsibility, to develop their professional
competence, and assist others in the care team, including informal carers,
to contribute safely and to a degree appropriate to their roles.

The traditional approach to teaching and assessing has been to impose a clearly defined body of knowledge and practical expertise on the student which is then assessed in a somewhat impersonal and authoritarian manner. The hierarchical structure of the nursing profession (see p. 58) tends to perpetuate such methods and attitudes and in spite of changing techniques, the power is seen to be firmly in the hands of the teacher and assessor. The law also emphasises the authority of these roles, but this chapter will show that through both employment legislation and the law on negligence, the learner on the receiving end also has some rights and means of redress.

Who are the learners?

Students undertaking statutory training for the various parts of the Register at present make up the bulk of learners (see p. 44), both in numbers entering such training and because of the length of their courses. However, many registered nurses proceed to approved shorter courses in specialist areas, for example, theatre, renal, intensive care and oncology nursing. Community nurse training takes place in colleges of further education, but clinical placements are still required and teachers of nurses also need to learn how to teach.

Apart from such statutory and approved courses, there is the important area of inservice training. The vital nature of this for such topics as lifting and handling patients, dealing with violence and preventing cross-infection has been discussed in Chapter 10. In addition increasing the scope of professional practice and management training is often dealt with within the organisation. Thus all registered nurses are likely at some time in their careers to be learners and therefore be the object of teaching and assessing.

As was pointed out in Chapter 3 (p. 43), the Nurses Rules (1983) provide a legal framework controlling statutory trainings. The National Boards have to approve these trainings and a specific requirement exists for registration in relation to assessment:

> To qualify as a person who can apply to be registered in one or more of Parts 1 to 8 of the Register, a student shall
>
> (i) have her name on the index of students maintained by a Board
>
> (ii) have completed the relevant training required
>
> (iii) have passed an examination held or arranged by a Board . . . which shall be designed so as to assess the student's theoretical knowledge, practical skills and attitudes and demonstrate her ability to undertake the relevant competencies specified in Rule 18 of these rules. (Section 19)

The importance of applying knowledge and skills is also highlighted in the amendment rules (1989) covering Project 2000 training. This document also lays down the requirement that 'the assignment of appropriate duties to others and the supervision, teaching and monitoring of assigned duties' is one of the outcomes required for registration on Part 12, 13, 14 or 15 of the Register.

Many areas of nursing require knowledge and skill beyond the requirements of basic training and the assessment of competence in these areas becomes an important legal issue (see p. 61). In addition, for some inservice training the legal framework is given by the Health and Safety at Work Act. As clause 14 of the Code points out, informal carers, as part of the care team, may also be in the position of learners. The legal framework for this is particularly highlighted on p. 72.

Who are the teachers and assessors?

The Nurses Rules (Section 11) lay down a number of additional qualifications that will be recorded on the Register and these include teachers of nursing, teachers of midwifery and teachers of health visiting. Such entries 'shall only be made in respect of persons whose name appears in a Part or Parts of the Register'.

The registered nurse tutor or clinical teacher, as well as having successfully completed a specific training programme in education, must also be a professionally experienced nurse. The Boards spell out criteria regarding the number of years' experience since registration as well as academic achievement required for a nurse to become a teacher of nursing. Approval of an institution for training purposes will require that a large proportion of the teachers are fully qualified and registered for that function.

Great reliance is put on clinical staff to perform a teaching function for learners gaining experience in their ward, department or community patch. Short teaching and assessing courses need to be provided, either on an inservice basis or as an approved course. Legally, responsibility for teaching and assessing is part of a number of nurses' contracts under the clinical grading system. Scales D–G inclusive cover aspects of supervision and teaching of both unqualified and qualified staff. A post-holder at Scale D may 'be required to demonstrate procedures to and supervise qualified and/or unqualified staff' and the responsibilities of a member of staff at Scale G include 'the teaching of staff and/or students' (DHSS 1988).

For statutory trainings, examinations have been devolved onto the training institution. This has led to the establishment of Examination Boards for the setting of examinations or assessments and the ratification of results. Again, the rules drawn up by the institution regarding the conduct and content of examinations and assessments are subject to the approval of the appropriate National Board. The inclusion of service representatives is considered important to reinforce and validate the links between theoretical and practical assessment. With the approval of many courses now at diploma level, the rules and regulations of Higher Education within a rather different statutory framework have to be integrated with professional requirements.

What is taught and learnt?

The student is entitled to the best instruction available. The legal implication of the teacher omitting to give certain information or of giving wrong information is potential negligence. This has become an issue in the training given in lifting and handling of patients. When a nurse with a back injury sues the health authority for negligence, part of the case is often based on the failure of the health authority to provide proper training. This may be because no teacher was allocated this task or the teachers giving such instruction failed to do so adequately, thus taking a share of the negligence. If there is no teacher skilled in giving the proper instruction, the employer has a legal duty to provide the expertise from outside the organisation if necessary.

This example is probably the only one in nurse training that has been tested in the courts. However, the potential for negligence exists whenever a failure in instruction clearly jeopardises the safety of the nurse being instructed or of the patient in her care. The importance of documenting training under the Health and Safety at Work Act has already been emphasised (p. 145) and this applies for all trainings, statutory and non-statutory. A lack of evidence of what teaching was given may well go in the plaintiff's favour (see p. 33).

Traditional methods of teaching are gradually being supplemented by newer ideas such as contract learning. The nature of this type of contract bears some resemblance to a legal contract (see p. 39) as it is an agreement between tutor and student that the student will commit herself to the achievement of certain learning objectives and the tutor will give certain specified help. However, such a contract cannot guarantee that learning takes place, but the student may have some cause to complain if the tutor, for no good reason, fails to give the support promised. Whether this has legal implications has yet to be demonstrated.

The assessment process

As Section 19 of the Nurses Rules points out, assessment of knowledge, skills and attitudes must demonstrate the nurse's abilities. Evidence of how this is to be done is required by the National Boards in order to give approval to a course. The details of how competence is to be assessed will include several components. Assessment strategies should show a clear link with the competencies to be achieved and a strong relationship between theory and practice (Rowntree 1977). Details of the appointment, preparation and monitoring of assessors is vital and policies and procedures related to the assessment process must be stated.

The English National Board has published a glossary of terms to assist in the formulation of valid assessment procedures and although these definitions are always open to argument, their use will assist in developing strategies that are likely to meet with approval. Those with potential legal significance are quoted below:

1. 'Assessment – the procedure by which a student is judged to have achieved the standard required for qualification.'
2. 'Supervision – the professional support of a student by appropriately qualified staff to facilitate developing competence in the practice of nursing.'
3. 'Competences – the ability to perform a particular activity to a prescribed standard.'
4. 'Assessor – an appropriately qualified and experienced first-level nurse who has undertaken a course to develop her skills in assessing or judging the students' level of attainment relating to the stated learning outcomes. The role of the assessor is a formal one. Each student is required to have an assessor or named assessor as appropriate.'
5. 'Supervisor – an appropriately qualified and experienced first-level nurse who has received preparation for ensuring that relevant experience is provided for students to enable learning outcomes to be achieved and for facilitating the students' developing competence in the practice of nursing by overseeing this practice. The role of the supervisor is a formal one and is normally included in the individual's managerial responsibilities. Each student is required to have a known supervisor on each shift when on duty.'
6. 'Mentor – an appropriately qualified and experienced first level nurse who, by example and facilitation, guides, assists and supports the student in learning new skills, adopting new behaviours and acquiring new attitudes.'
7. 'Formative assessment – continuing and systematic appraisal of a student to determine the degree of mastery of a given learning task and help the student and teacher to focus on particular learning necessary to achieve mastery.'
8. 'Summative assessment – a more general assessment of the extent to which a student has achieved outcomes/objectives for the course as a whole or a substantial part of it – contrib-

utes to the grading of a student, her qualification or certification.' (ENB 1988a)

In addition to guidelines, the National Boards also publish regulations giving some more precise details of how examinations and assessments are to be carried out (ENB 1988b). These regulations, although not carrying the full weight of the law as do the Nurses Rules, require compliance for two reasons; first, approval as a training institution is dependent on this; and secondly, an appeal by a student who failed to pass the training assessments or examinations would probably succeed if it was found that these had not been carried out in the required manner.

Employment legislation and assessment

The safety of patients must always be seen as the major concern of any employer and for this reason it is important that, if the employee proves to be unsafe or incompetent, dismissal on the grounds of misconduct can follow. It is within this context that the assessment of the majority of students has to take place. The assessment tool therefore has to build in criteria for discontinuation of training that safeguard the patient, protect other nurses but are at the same time fair to the student. The rules governing this process are based on employment legislation (see p. 3).

Methods of assessment will vary considerably from one training to another (Young 1980, 1982a). Where theoretical assessment is concerned, the usual pattern is to discontinue training after failure at a second attempt of an assessment or examination. The grounds for discontinuation on practical assessment may be based on a simple achievement/non-achievement of specified learning outcomes, or a more complex grading system (see Table 11.1). Whatever is used, there is a need to build in a second chance in order to give the student an opportunity to improve. It should also be specified in the associated assessment rules how the disciplinary machinery is to be implemented in the event of unsatisfactory performance. There will normally be a move from informal warning if the nature of the poor performance is not too severe, to formal warning if this continues or directly to formal warning if it is clearly unsafe behaviour. For example, a student who has difficulty in organising her work may initially receive an informal warning and counselling, whereas a marked failure to understand and respond to nursing instructions may necessitate moving directly to a formal disciplinary situation. Continuing poor performance may finally lead to discontinuation.

It is important not to allow the incompetent student to remain in training for a prolonged period, thereby putting patients at risk. On the other hand, there is a conflict in the shorter trainings between giving the student sufficient time to improve and protecting the public by discontinuing employment before the student finishes the course. The student's manager in this employment situation is always the educational institution, not the service nurse, although she has to take some responsibility for the assessment process. It is therefore the tutorial staff who initiate any

I	A	B	C	D
Recognise when a patient is potentially at risk due to his condition	Very perceptive and ready to act	Recognises potential risks but needs guidance on action to be taken	Often needs reminding of potential risks	Lacks awareness unless very obvious
Be responsible for writing reports on patient care	Writes clearly and concisely, always accurate	Writes relevant report, usually clearly	Sometimes reports written inaccurately	Reports tend to be inadequate and poorly presented
Able to make the patient comfortable	Maintains the comfort of the patient at all times	Usually maintains the comfort of the patient	Does not pay enough attention to detail in order to maintain patient's comfort	Is unable to maintain the comfort of the patient

| Satisfactory | Unsatisfactory |

II		
Identify patients at risk of developing secondary complications, e.g. pressure sores, delayed wound healing, chest infections, low mood	Achieved	Not achieved
Contribute to the accurate and up-to-date records of nursing with due regard to confidentiality	Achieved	Not achieved
Demonstrate skill in making a patient feel relaxed and comfortable	Achieved	Not achieved

Table 11.1 Two samples of practical assessment procedures

disciplinary procedures resulting from poor assessment, although they cannot carry this out effectively if the service staff who have been assessors and supervisors have not completed the following:

- the documents used are signed and dated,
- sufficient detail is given of why the assessment was unsatisfactory,
- the assessment was discussed with the student,
- remedial help was offered to the student.

It is also useful for the tutor to know if there are any other relevant factors, such as student sickness, which may have affected performance. It is not up to the service staff to let such information condone a poor performance. The tutor will be the person to assess the relevance of such information and in all disciplinary procedures must be able to rely on the honesty and professional standards of the assessors. Failure to give a poor assessment when it is justified in order to be kind does not protect patients or uphold professional standards.

Because of the legal framework, a student who is dismissed because of poor performance has the right of appeal. Within the first two years of employment, this is limited. The student cannot take the appeal to health authority level or to industrial tribunal. However, it is only students in some of the statutory trainings who will be limited in this way. Students undertaking a second statutory qualification or a post-basic course will have this right immediately, even if they are only recently employed by that particular health authority.

A student who is not also an employee – for example, students undertaking a college-based course on a grant or Project 2000 training – will not have the protection of employment legislation. However, for the gaining of clinical experience, the health authority needs to supply some kind of honorary contract. It is therefore good practice to draw up clear rules which are fair to both parties when performance is unsatisfactory even if such rules are not legally required.

Negligence and assessment

The potential negligence of the unqualified nurse and of the nurse delegating care to her has been discussed in some depth (Chapter

4, pp. 55–58). This area of the law is particularly relevant to the assessment and supervision of the student and the main points are summarised below.

1. The student has to be legally responsible for the care she gives; she cannot plead ignorance or lack of experience if giving unsafe or poor quality care. Therefore she must acknowledge her limitations and seek help when necessary.
2. The student should always be working under supervision and should be informed of this. The degree of supervision legally required will decrease as the competence of the student increases but will still exist until the point of qualification is reached.
3. Delegation of work to the student must consider safety and include an assessment of the student's knowledge and skill as well as the ongoing supervision as mentioned in (2).

More recent developments in practical assessment have tended to put more emphasis on the two-way process between assessor and student. However, in any assessment scheme there must be a core of objectives related to safe care that cannot be open to negotiation.

Assessment of health care assistants

With the implementation of Project 2000 training, the importance of a support worker role to the registered nurse was recognised. Unqualified nurses, the nursing auxiliaries, were rarely given anything but minimal training. The support worker or health care assistant is trained and assessed in a much more systematic way using the framework of NVQs (national vocational qualifications) (NCVQ 1991). The award of an NVQ is based on the assessment of competence at a certain level and the following definitions are a general guide:

Level 1. competence in the performance of a range of varied work activities, most of which may be routine and predictable.
Level 2. competence in a significant range of varied work activities, performed in a variety of contexts. Some of the activities are complex or non-routine, and there is some individual responsibility or autonomy. Collaboration with others, perhaps through membership of a work group or team, may often be a requirement.

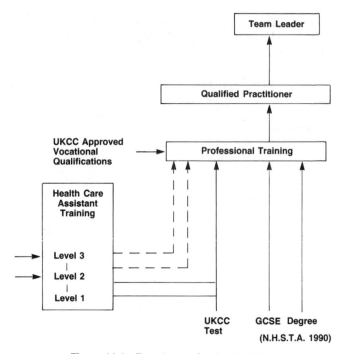

Figure 11.1 Entry into professional training

Level 3. competence in a broad range of varied work activities performed in a wide variety of contexts and most of which are complex and non-routine. There is considerable responsibility and autonomy, and control or guidance of others is often required.

Level 3 is usually seen as the point of entry into professional training (Figure 11.1). The qualification can be awarded by a number of official bodies. All of these have strict criteria for the appointment of assessors who must undertake training and regular updating in order to take on this role.

Assessment of trained staff

Assessments of trained staff – usually called appraisal systems or individual performance reviews – contain some elements in common with assessment of learners. They aim to identify key tasks and specify objectives that the member of staff intends to achieve. There is usually a greater responsibility put on the employee to share in the formulation of these objectives but these must then be agreed by the person's manager and therefore be acceptable to the overall aims of the organisation.

The nurse being appraised may find the process uncomfortable rather than helpful. There is always the anxiety that it will be used to criticise some failure and that this in due course may lead to the use of the disciplinary procedure against her. There is, of course, some truth in this if performance is unsatisfactory. As has been pointed out, the employer has the right to terminate a person's employment on the grounds of misconduct. However, a regular (e.g. annual) appraisal interview has as its main function the development of the staff member towards a greater potential.

Where the appraisal may be used as part of a disciplinary process, this should be quite clear to the nurse as it will be initiated as a result of some criticism of the nurse's performance. As in the case of students, any kind of warning under the disciplinary policy must include an opportunity to improve before dismissal can occur.

Defamation and assessment

The assessor may be concerned that if she writes a poor report on the person being assessed she may be accused of libel and if she makes adverse verbal comments, the charges might be slander. However, as with writing about patients (see p. 114), there is unlikely to be defamation as long as what the assessor writes or says is true and privilege is maintained, that is, the information is only divulged to the proper people such as the immediate manager or tutor (Young 1982b).

A precaution to take in making statements about a person's performance is to avoid using extreme language as this would be less likely to be believed in a court case than more moderate statements. For example, it is wise to write 'usually', 'tends to', 'as far as can be judged', instead of 'always' or 'is'. Any statements concerning dishonesty or untrustworthiness must be supported by definite proof. If these guidelines are followed, the assessor should not fear any threats to sue that may be made in the heat of the moment.

The writing of references may also have legal implications. As the

Key task no.	Key tasks	Standards of performance	Description of action plans	Date action plan		Action required by manager	Progress, success or failure	Suggestions for improving job
				Set	Com-pleted			

Figure 11.2 Sample staff development and performance review form

privilege existing usually means that the person on whom it is written will not have access to its contents, the writer need not fear an action for defamation. However, a referee can be negligent if failing to give accurate information, either good or bad. In *Lawton* v. *BOC Transhield Ltd* 1986, negligence was upheld when an employee lost his new job as a result of an inaccurate, unfavourable reference. Similarly, a false good reference that then led to patients being harmed as a result of the new employee being incompetent would also be negligence on the part of the referee.

Conclusion

There is a number of legal implications for employer, teacher, assessor and learner in the performance of their roles. On the whole the law is concerned with ensuring safety of the patient and the rights of the student must be secondary. From the professional point of view, this is usually accepted as necessary. Although Clause 14 of the Code of Professional Conduct puts the emphasis on caring for colleagues, such concern must be seen as just one part of the nurse's overall legal and professional responsibilities.

The following story provides a postscript. A student nurse had been near to dismissal on several occasions during her training due to a failure to achieve the necessary level of competence. However, the disciplinary process allowed the learner extra opportunities to improve and on each occasion the student managed to lift her performance sufficiently to be allowed to continue. By the end of training the student was allowed to register although doubts were expressed by the tutorial staff as to the efficiency of the assessment process that allowed such a student to complete training.

There was one area in which this student excelled and that was theatre nursing. The newly qualified nurse was strongly recommended to apply for a theatre job, which she did. The reference, while expressing honest doubts as to her competence in other areas, was able to support this application. The nurse subsequently made a successful career in theatre nursing.

References

Department of Health and Social Security 1988. *New Clinical Grading Structure for Nurses, Midwives and Health Visitors*, EL(88)P33. DHSS, London.

English National Board 1988a. *Institutional and Course Approval/Reapproval Process: information required, criteria and guidelines*, Circular 1988/39/APS. ENB, London.

English National Board 1988b. *Regulations for the Conduct of Courses Leading to Admission to Parts 1–8 of the Professional Register and Postbasic Courses*, Circular 1988/52/APS. ENB, London.

National Council for Vocational Qualifications 1991. *The NCVQ Framework*. NCVQ, Department of Employment, London.

NHS Training Authority 1990. *Support Workers/Helpers: The Way Forward*. NHSTA, Department of Health, London.

Rowntree D 1977. *Assessing Students. How shall we know them?* Harper & Row, London.

Statutory Instruments 1983. *Nurses, Midwives and Health Visitors Rules*. Approval Order No. 873. HMSO, London.

Statutory Instrument 1989. *Nurses, Midwives and Health Visitors (training amendment rules)*. Approval Order No. 1456. HMSO, London.

Young A P 1980. Progress and problems of continuous assessment. Occasional Paper. *Nursing Times* **758**(8), pp. 33–5.

Young A P 1982a. Measurement of nursing skills – the search for a suitable assessment tool. Occasional Paper. *Nursing Times* **78**(15), pp. 57–60.

Young A P 1982b. Reports and references. *Nursing*, 1st series, **36**, April, pp. 1547–8.

CHAPTER 12

Exerting Undue Influence

Refuse any gift, favour or hospitality from patients or clients currently in your care which might be interpreted as seeking to exert influence to obtain preferential consideration.

Ensure that your registration status is not used in the promotion of commercial products or services, declare any financial or other interests in relevant organisations providing such goods or services and ensure that your professional judgment is not influenced by any commercial considerations.

I swear by Apollo the healer and Aesculapius and Hygeia and All-heal (Panacea) and all the gods and goddesses . . . that according to my ability and judgement, I will keep this oath . . . to teach this Art without fee or stipulation. . . . I will follow that system of regimen which, according to my ability and judgement, I consider for the benefit of my patients and abstain from whatever is deleterious and mischievous. Into whatsoever houses I enter, I will go there for the benefit of the sick and will abstain from every act of mischief and corruption. (part of the Hippocratic Oath, cited in Mason and McCall-Smith 1987)

The independence and impartiality of the professional is seen as an important characteristic to the public. They have come to rely on and trust a high degree of morality in the dealings of doctors and nurses, contrasting this with the view that many businesses, or even other public offices, are not immune from corruption. However, a number of pressures are put on professionals that do not always make it easy to keep to such a high standard. Although the law to some extent supports the professional, current changes in political attitudes towards and administrative practices in the

National Health Service to make it more like a business may almost unwittingly alter the professional's behaviour.

Accepting money and gifts

Gifts may be offered to nurses by patients, colleagues and external agencies. Although the significance of these offerings may vary, the underlying legal position is the same for all of them. The background legislation is the Prevention of Corruption Acts 1906 and 1916 which specifically include persons 'serving under the Crown'. In order to clarify this legislation for staff in the National Health Service, the Department of Health and Social Security issued a draft health notice on 'Acceptance of funding, gifts and hospitality and declaration of interest' (1985). It states:

> It is a basic principle in all parts of the public service that public servants must be scrupulously impartial and honest, that they must be seen to be so and that they must be beyond the reach of suspicion.

The Corruption Acts 1906 and 1916 prohibit staff from obtaining or seeking to obtain in their private or official capacity any gifts or consideration of any kind from contractors or individuals with whom they are in contact through their employment where these may be an inducement or reward for acting or refraining from acting in a certain way, or for showing favour or disfavour to any person. The legal outcomes for being in breach of these Acts could be prosecution, dismissal and for the nurse, removal from the Register. In addition, there is the possibility of accusations of theft if a gift is later regretted.

The majority of nurses are offered gifts by patients as an expression of their gratitude. Patients are often very insistent and the nurse may feel that to refuse would cause hurt and embarrassment. The Prevention of Corruption Act 1906 refers to 'any gift or consideration' and goes on to define consideration to include 'valuable consideration of any kind'. Therefore, if the gift is not valuable, the nurse can feel confident that accepting it would not lay her open to a charge of bribery or corruption. However, if her health authority has a strict policy of not accepting *any* gift, she must abide by this or face disciplinary action. Even small gifts can cause later problems if the patient is confused. The patient may forget that she has given a treasured trinket to the nurse and become upset, and this may also make the relatives angry. If in doubt or if the patient is over-insistent, the nurse would be wise to refer the patient to her manager.

Another situation that arises is when a patient gives a nurse money to buy some shopping for her. Usually this is for small items such as soap or stamps, but even such small errands may make the nurse vulnerable to later accusations of theft. Such errands are not the responsibility of the nurse so she has no obligation to undertake them. But if, as a personal favour, she chooses to help the patient in this way, she would be wiser to buy the items with her own money and then present the patient with a receipt in order to be reimbursed.

When the patient is mentally incapacitated, the nurse is put into a further dilemma. A long-stay patient can accumulate considerable money from unspent pension or social security benefit. The decision as to how to spend this money may be left with the nurse (Hodges 1991). Spending it on treats for the patient seems acceptable. Using the money for equipment or refurbishment could be seen as mismanagement of patients' funds. The nurse will need to order the goods which the patient is most likely to appreciate and the nurse in charge of each ward should maintain for inspection by a senior nurse a simple record of all goods obtained for individual patients or held in the ward on their behalf. Scottish guidelines state that patients should be encouraged to spend their income on items not normally provided by the NHS and decisions should be taken by a multidisciplinary team. Such advice seems sensible on a professional level.

Nurses are also offered gifts from external agencies, for example, pharmaceutical companies. Although such gifts may be offered 'without strings', acceptance may create a sense of obligation which could affect future impartiality. The general principle to be followed is not to accept anything which may, or may be thought likely to, influence a purchasing decision. Nurses may feel that there are no adverse effects to accepting a diary or pen, but they should remain alert to any potential inducements and if suspicious of the external agencies' intentions, should report them to their manager. Staff should be aware that health authorities are required to insert in every formal contract to purchase a clause entitling them to cancel the contract and recover any losses if any inducements or gifts are offered by the contractor.

External agencies sometimes offer certain services to staff free, for example lectures or training sessions covering a wider remit than the use of their product. Hospitality and the funding of conferences are other offers made by commercial concerns. The same criteria apply in these situations as mentioned above. A precaution to take would be to inform one's manager and to check that the content of lecture or conference is confined to professional and educational matters before taking up such an offer.

Wills and the dying patient

A special circumstance, which may trigger accusations of the nurse applying undue pressure on another individual, is in the making of a will. It is not unusual for a person who is seriously ill suddenly to realise the importance of organising his affairs and the person most immediately to hand is the nurse. If possible, the nurse should avoid being involved, to avoid subsequent accusations of undue pressure and because certain legal requirements must be observed for a will to be valid (Pritchard 1984).

The testator must be over eighteen years and of sound mind. Foolishness, eccentricity or social pressure are not enough to invalidate a will but fear, fraud or coercion will do so and, if there is a suspicion that a nurse has applied any pressure to benefit under her patient's will, the gift may be disallowed.

In England, Wales and Northern Ireland, the will must be signed by the person making the will in the presence of two witnesses who must also sign in each other's presence at the same time. If the nurse is to benefit under the will, she cannot be a witness to it, or, if she is, then the part of the will making her a beneficiary becomes invalid. A husband or wife cannot act as a witness to their spouse's will.

In Scotland there are several differences. If a patient cannot sign, a solicitor, Justice of the Peace, or minister of the parish can sign on his behalf. The witnesses need not sign at the same time provided they saw the patient sign the will or heard him acknowledge his signature and provided they sign before his death. Additionally, a witness may benefit under the will. Finally, a paper called a holograph can be written by a person without witnesses and, as long as it is in his own handwriting and dated and signed by him, it is likely to be accepted as long as the bequests are straightforward.

The hospital nurse should be able to obtain the services of an

This is the last Will and Testament

of me ....

of ....

in the County of ....made this ....

day of ....in the year of our Lord one thousand nine

hundred and ....

    I HEREBY revoke all former Wills, Codicils and other Testamentary instruments made by me and

declare this to be my last Will. I appoint ....

....

to be my Executor(s) and direct that all my debts and Funeral Expenses shall be paid as soon as convenient

after my death.

    I GIVE AND BEQUEATH unto

....

....

....

....

....

....

....

....

....

....

....

....

....

....

....

....

....

....

Signed by the said TESTATOR
in the presence of us, present at the same time, who at
h   request, in h   presence, and in the presence of
each other, have subscribed our names as witnesses.
    If necessary to use next page, strike this out

Figure 12.1a Sample form of will

DIRECTIONS

1.   The Testator is the person who makes the Will.

2.   Write plainly and concisely the manner in which you desire to dispose of your property. Use plain words and avoid legal phrases, or words which you do not understand.

3.   Attend particularly to the legal formalities required in the execution of the Will.

4.   Do not attempt to make a Codicil to your Will, that is an addition or alteration of its provisions. It is better to re-write a Will than alter it. No stamp is required on a Will.

5.   Persons under the age of eighteen years cannot make a Will (in Scotland a girl over 12 or a boy over 14 can make a Will). All property can be disposed of by a Will.

6.   Every Will should be signed by the Testator; such signature must be in the presence of at least two witnesses who must also sign their names, before either leaves the Testator's presence. It is not necessary that the witnesses should know the contents of the Will, all they have to do is witness the Testator's signature. The Testator should sign immediately below the last line of the Will; anything after the signature may be invalid.

7.   Against every alteration or interlineation made before the Will is executed, the Testator and the Witness must sign their initials or names, and the fact of their having been made should be noted in the attestation clause. But when possible it is better to re-write a Will then to have any alterations in it. Nothing should be scratched out or erased or the Will might be invalidated.

8.   Persons who take anything under a Will should not be witnesses, as bequests made to them would be invalid. The wife or husband of a person who takes anything under a Will should not be a witness, as the gift would be altogether void. Executors should not witness a Will, as any bequest made to them would then be void.

9.   A legacy to a friend is made void by his death before the Testator's.

10.   A legacy to a Testator's child or other issue does not lapse by his death if he has any issue living at the time of the Testator's death, but the legacy takes effect as one to the issue of the predeceased child living at the Testator's death.

11.   A soldier (including a member of the air force) and a mariner or seaman at sea, although under twenty-one years of age, can dispose of his real and personal property by any written paper signed by him, though not attested, providing in the case of a soldier or member of the air force there is a state of war either actual of threatened and the Testator, in his capacity as a member of the Forces is somewhere for the purposes of that war.

12.(a) In some circumstances a Will made before a marriage may continue to be valid, but we suggest a new Will should be made.

12.(b) Where after a Testator has made a Will his or her marriage ends in divorce or is annulled it is best to make a new Will.

13.   After a Will has been duly executed, no addition to, or alteration in it, may be made. It should be kept in a safe place and the Executor informed where it can be found.

14.   If a Testator has any interest in a Trust or Settlement of which he can dispose by Will or wishes to create any Trust by his Will it is recommended he should consult a s solicitor before making his Will.

15.   Before proving a Will the executors should purchase a small book entitled "How to prove a Will" price £1.50 (including Postage), to be had from Alfred Hinde Printer, Publishing House, Saltwells Road, Netherton, Dudley, or any Bookseller by means of which they will be able to prove a Will without legal aid.

Figure 12.1b   Directions for making a will

administrator if a patient requests her help in this matter. Even outside office hours, someone should be on call. The community nurse is in a more isolated situation and may have to act as a witness.

She should note the points mentioned above. A sample form of will is shown in Figure 12.1.

Advertising and the law

The function of advertising is to inform and persuade. It is therefore a way in which undue influence can be exerted by one person or organisation on another. When the advertisement is limited to the giving of information, its effect on attitudes is likely to be minimal. However, if information is being given by a *nurse*, the image created may be emotive and therefore again over-influence the customer.

Traditionally, the advertising industry has been allowed to police itself through self-regulatory controls rather than statutory ones. (Williams and Samuels 1979). However, the content of advertising must not violate a number of statutes. The most important of these is the Trades Description Act 1968 which stipulates that all descriptions of goods in advertising must be legally accurate under the Act. Criminal prosecution, usually by the Trading Standards Officer, can follow if these conditions are flouted.

Other statutes related to advertising practice that are relevant to nurses are the Adoption Act 1958 which restricts advertisements concerned with the adoption of children and the Children Act 1958 which prohibits anonymous advertisements offering to undertake care of children. The Cancer Act 1939 forbids the advertising of any offer to treat, prescribe for or advise on cancer and the Venereal Diseases Act 1917 also controls advertising treatment in this area. Hearing aid dispensers and opticians are restricted in their advertising (Hearing Aid Council Act 1968 and Opticians Act 1958) and advertisements for medicines must conform to certain terms, with penalties for misleading advertising (Medicines Act 1968).

Advertising and the nurse

The nurse may wish to advertise her services as a nurse for a number of different reasons. She may be working independently as a private nurse, she may own a business such as a nursing home or she may be employed as a nurse for a company promoting particular products.

Legally the restraints are minimal. Claiming to be a nurse for the purpose of selling her services or products if she is not, in fact, on the Register could flout the Trades Description Act. Apart from that there are only a few areas of medicine and health care with limited advertising freedom. However, professionally, the nurse should restrict herself to information giving rather than using undue influence. The United Kingdom Central Council has published a notice with additional information to the person advertising as a nurse. It states that this is acceptable provided that the advertisement:

- 'is not ostentatious' and
- 'does not make claims that the practitioner is to be preferred over others' (1985).

Where advertising has as its function the promotion of a commercial product, any nurse who has been involved in providing material should not have her registration status stated by her name in any acknowledgements. However, if the material is educational or documentary, the UKCC states that in this situation an indication of the nurse's registration status is acceptable. The UKCC is adamant that nurses must not use their registration when advertising for work in some other sphere where registration is not a requirement.

The final comment on the UKCC (1985) notice on advertising states:

> The indication of a person's registration status as a nurse, midwife or health visitor outside the above stated tolerances may be regarded as unacceptable and result in charges of misconduct.

A more subtle form of advertising takes place as follows. Some nurses were asked by a charity to assist in fund-raising and it was requested they wear their uniforms while doing so. It was obviously felt that if nurses were seen to be supporting this charity, it would encourage the public to contribute. This unspoken form of advertising is not illegal. The only constraint would be if the health authority's uniform policy stated specifically that uniform was not to be worn away from the place of work or was only to be worn on duty. In such a case the nurses involved could be disciplined for their actions. The way around this would be for the employer to be approached for permission. The charity may be one that the health authority would wish to support or even be specifically for the benefit of patients in their care. A statement from the UKCC (1990) points out that the use of professional uniforms to carry advertising through the use of emblems or other embellishments for commercial promotion is not acceptable.

Marketing health services

The National Health Service is being expected to act on more businesslike lines than ever before (see p. 171):

> It is clear that the organisation of the NHS. . . . needs to be reformed. The Government has been tackling these organisational problems and has taken a series of measures to improve the way the NHS is managed. The main one was the introduction of general management from 1984. This is now showing results and has pointed the way ahead. (Working for Patients 1989, Section 1.5)

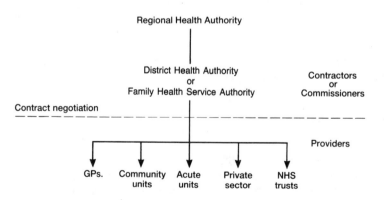

Figure 12.2 Simplified model of provision of services in the NHS

Under the NHS and Community Care Act 1990, the structure of the NHS is divided into commissioners and providers of care (see Figure 12.2). The providers of health care services are in a contractual relationship with District and Regional Health Authorities or Family Health Service Authorities.

This model introduces the likelihood of competition for contracts, particularly with the District Health Authority.

> The Government believes that the primary task of each DHA should be to secure the best and most cost-effective services it can for its patients, whether or not those services are provided by the District's own hospitals. (Section 4.2)
>
> Similarly, the Government believes that NHS hospitals should be free to offer their services to their own Districts and to other Districts in a way which enables them to attract the funds they need in line with the work they are asked to do. (Section 4.3)

This statutory change has introduced a marketing orientation to the NHS whereas previously such an approach was only found in the private sector. Units are having to measure their services in terms of cost, an exercise that is new to most of them and for which the necessary financial and informational infrastructure is less than ideal. Inevitably nurses are caught up in this change and nurse managers are having to learn many new skills and a fresh orientation. Ensuring that her 'professional judgment is not influenced by any commercial considerations' is an increasingly difficult ideal for the nurse. The choices available to the nurse manager may be between commercial considerations ensuring the survival of her particular unit or ward, and the overall wider professional viewpoint of working towards the best good of the greatest number of patients. These are really ethical decisions rather than legal ones and the nurse has to balance her employment position against professional judgment.

Conflict of interests

A number of other commercial pressures can be imposed on nurses. Some find that their posts are either totally or partly funded by private sponsorship. Nurses in this position need to ensure that their professional judgment is not compromised, for example by limiting their freedom of choice when deciding what products to buy or recommend to their clients. Specialist nurses are in a particularly vulnerable position, for example nurses involved in stomas, breastcare and diabetes. They should look carefully at the nature of the employment contract offered and take further advice if unsure of the wording of some clauses.

As nurses are more often involved with holding budgets, the possibility of influence being exerted on them in the choice of products is increased. This can be quite legitimate but it does mean the nurse should be aware of the law on standards that must be met. The Consumer Protection Act 1987 creates a strict civil liability for damage caused by defective products. It is likely that the nurse should take certain safeguards in recording from whom and when a product was obtained and in ensuring that equipment is properly maintained and again that records are kept of this. Sound purchasing decisions and protocols will provide additional help in preventing later legal problems.

Nurses who are working with the elderly or mentally ill must ensure that they are not influenced by commercial considerations if involved with assessing and advising clients and their families on suitable residential accommodation. Cases have been known of nurses having a financial interest in a nursing home and allowing this to influence the manner in which patients are directed. Guidelines from the Department of Health are awaited.

Conclusion

The law to some extent supports the professional view that there must be limitations on the influence exerted on and by nurses. The independence of the professional and the trust of the public are seen as important in a number of legal areas and in addition a failure to abide by clauses fifteen and sixteen of the Code of Professional Conduct can lead to charges of misconduct. It seems likely that this is an area where it may become increasingly difficult to maintain high professional standards and therefore one on which all nurses need to reflect.

References

Department of Health and Social Security 1985. *Acceptance of Funding, Gifts and Hospitality and Declaration of Interest*. Draft Health Notice. DHSS, London.
Hodges P 1991. Cash points. *Nursing Times* **87** (17), 24 April, p. 20.
Mason J K and McCall-Smith A (1987) *Law and Medical Ethics*, 2nd edition. Butterworth, London.
Pritchard J 1984. *The Penguin Guide to the Law*. Penguin Books, Harmondsworth, Middlesex.
United Kingdom Central Council 1985. *Advertising*. UKCC, London.
United Kingdom Central Council 1992. *Code of Professional Conduct for the Nurse, Midwife and Health Visitor*, 3rd edition. UKCC, London.

United Kingdom Central Council 1990. *Statement on Advertising and Commercial Sponsorship*. UKCC, London.

White Paper 1989. *Working for Patients*. HMSO, London.

Williams J and Samuels I 1979. Marketing and advertising. In *Managing Your Business Guides: Selling, Importing and Exporting*. Hamlyn, London.

Changing the Law

To quite a marked extent, professional conduct has a sound legal base and there are occasions when a knowledge of the law can actually assist the nurse in areas of professional difficulty or potential conflict. However, the reader may well conclude that there is a number of situations where the law provides rather minimal support for the nurse in carrying out her professional responsibilities and even a few areas where it is downright unhelpful.

The law is not a fixed entity but an evolving institution. It can be changed in a number of ways.

Statute law

An Act of Parliament officially begins with a Bill (Padfield 1983). However, a number of stages may precede the presentation of a Bill to Parliament. A Green Paper may be published by the Government to test public opinion, followed by a White Paper which states the Government's intentions in the proposed area of legislation. In 1989, the White Paper *Working with Patients* on the restructuring of the National Health Service was published without a preceding Green Paper, giving less time for public response.

There are two types of Bill, the majority of which are Government Bills. There is a tremendous pressure on parliamentary time to take these Bills through the procedures required for them to become Acts. It is therefore not surprising that the second type – Private Member's Bills – are much less likely to become law due to lack of time unless the Government specifically supports them. In 1988, a Bill introduced by David Alton to reduce the time-limit for legal abortion failed for this reason. It was fairly easy for those against the Bill to use delaying tactics to ensure that the time allocated to debating the Bill was insufficient.

There are set stages through which a Bill must pass (see Figure C.1). On its introduction in the House of Commons the Bill receives its first reading at which it is not read at all. This stage is used to inform Members of Parliament that the Bill is published. The second reading is the stage at which the main points are debated and, if it survives, it passes to committee stage. A Standing Committee consists of members (usually 15–20) chosen in proportionate numbers with those of the main parties in the House of Commons. Amendments are proposed and voted on. The Bill then returns to the House for its Report Stage when the amendments are debated. The Bill can be referred back to the Committee after this, then finally reaches its third reading. After passing this, it goes to the House of Lords for a similar procedure. The Lords can delay a Bill but cannot ultimately stop it if it is introduced on a further occasion. Once through the Lords, the Bill receives the Royal Assent and becomes an Act.

The public in general and the nursing profession in particular can influence statute law in several ways. First, it is important that it gives a response to any Green Papers and White Papers published and the format of the Bill may well show some response to comments received by the time it reaches its first reading. During the progress of a Bill through Parliament, further influence may be extended by individuals through their own Members of Parliament. Finally, the profession has the possibility of persuading a Member of Parliament to put forward a Private Member's Bill, although, as was stated above, the success of this route is limited. However, it can heighten public and political awareness of the need for legislation in a certain area. Again, the need to alter abortion time-limits is a good example. Late 1989 saw the introduction of the Government-supported Embryology Bill which includes a section relating to abortion.

Because of the time constraints in Parliament, much law is now enacted via delegated legislation, e.g. Statutory Instruments. The Nurses, Midwives and Health Visitors Act 1979 is the one best known to nurses to function in this way. The United Kingdom Central Council has the power to amend the Nurses Rules from time to time without going back to Parliament, although the appropriate Minister of State must authorise these changes. From the nurse's point of view the use of delegated legislation gives the profession greater control over its own affairs. The present composition of the UKCC also ensures that a number of views are

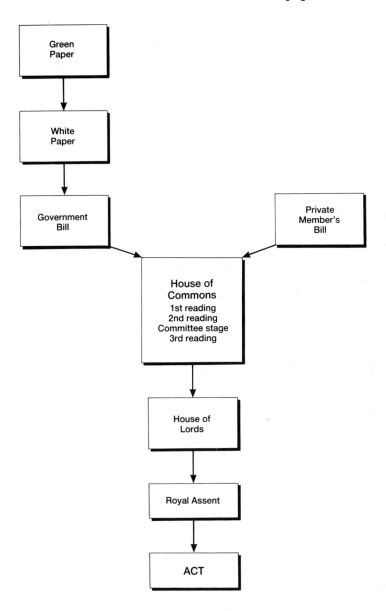

Figure C.1 The legislative process

represented and that the professional rights of those on the Register to be consulted are respected. For example, the Statutory Instruments amending the Nurses Rules to include Project 2000 followed a long period of discussion and review of the profession's opinions.

Case law

Case law constitutes a large amount of the law in the United Kingdom and is built up out of precedents (Eddey 1982). A precedent is a previous decision of a court which may be, in certain circumstances, binding on another court in deciding a similar case (the law in Scotland also uses certain legal principles). Which decisions are binding depends on the level of the court in which the decision was reached (see Figure C.2). Cases heard in the county courts and magistrates' courts (outer house of the Court of Session and Sheriff's Court in Scotland) are not generally reported and do not create binding precedents. However, the next level of court which hears appeals is bound by its own previous decisions unless the House of Lords, the final level of appeal, has ruled differently. Thus, following through the case initiated by Mrs Victoria Gillick in relation to advice and prescription of contraception to those under sixteen years (see p. 69), the original finding against Mrs Gillick was first overruled at appeal in her favour and then altered back to the original finding by the appeal judges of the House of Lords. This last finding stands and affects future cases.

A criticism of case law is that it is judge-made. As the majority of judges are male, white and middle-class, certain attitudes may tend to be perpetuated (Pattullo 1983). Case law can also be very unwieldy because of the number of reported cases and it may be rather slow to respond to social change. However, the advantages are to some extent the converse of these disadvantages. Social pressure can bring about change. The penalties being given to those convicted of rape have shown an increase in severity over recent years in line with public disgust at the way some judges were dealing with such cases. Also, although change may be slow, adaptation of the law to changing circumstances does occur.

If all this seems beyond the influence of the nursing profession, there is one way nurses influence case law and that is through the evidence they give as expert witnesses. The changing nature of nursing can be presented to a court in this way, clearing up old

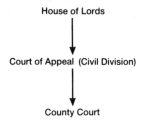

A. England, Wales and Northern Ireland

House of Lords

Court of Appeal (Civil Division)

County Court

B. Scotland

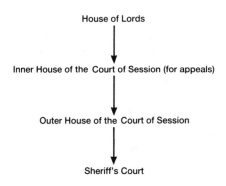

House of Lords

Inner House of the Court of Session (for appeals)

Outer House of the Court of Session

Sheriff's Court

Figure C.2   Precedence of the civil courts

misconceptions and forging links between what is acceptable to the profession and what is integrated into the law.

Nurses as a pressure group

As has been shown above, the most marked effect the public can have on the law is to influence the progress of parliamentary legislation. The individual alone is unlikely to have much effect, but a group of like-minded people who are also well organised may form a pressure group whom the Government or individual Members of Parliament may find difficult to ignore.

The medical profession has long had a marked influence on legislation affecting health matters. The general practitioner services reflect the success that this part of the medical profession has had in shaping its structure, although this is likely to be modified with recent contractual changes. The nursing profession, by contrast, has had less success in safeguarding its interests whenever reshaping of the health service or its own structure has occurred.

Several reasons underlie this failure of nurses to form successful pressure groups (Salvage 1985). First, nursing is traditionally female and passive (see p. 57) and although more men are now joining the nursing profession, nurses are on the whole uneasy in pressing for their own interests. Secondly, nurses do not present a united front. Many nurses recognise the importance of belonging to a union or professional body but do so mainly for legal protection. They may join one or two out of a possible twelve bodies, many of them not specifically for nurses or even for workers in the area of health care. This situation does not lead to great solidarity of nurses or presentation of a unanimous and forceful voice.

The onus is on individual nurses to become more politically aware and better organised if they wish to influence the law in the direction of greatest benefit to the profession and to the recipients of their care, the patients.

References

Eddey K 1982. *The English Legal System*, 3rd edition. Sweet & Maxwell, London.
Padfield C 1983. *Law Made Simple*, revised by F. E. Smith, 6th edition. Heinemann, London.
Pattullo P 1983. *Judging Women*. National Council for Civil Liberties, London.
Salvage J 1985. *The Politics of Nursing*. Heinemann Medical, London.
White Paper (1989) *Working with Patients*. HMSO, London.

Further Reading

Books

Age Concern 1988. *Living Will: Consent to Treatment*. Edward Arnold, London.

Baly M E 1984. *Professional Responsibility*, 2nd edition. John Wiley, Chicester.

Bayliss P F C 1987. *An Introduction to the Law Relating to the Health Care Professions*. Ravenswood, Beckenham.

Brazier M 1992. *Medicine, Patients and the Law*, 2nd edition. Penguin, Harmondsworth, Middlesex.

Brennan J L 1980. *Medico-Legal Problems in Hospital Practice*. Ravenswood, Beckenham.

Byrne P 1990. *Ethics and Law in Health Care and Research*. John Wiley, Chichester.

Carson D and Montgomery J 1989. *Nursing and the Law*. Macmillan, Basingstoke.

Dimond B 1990. *Legal Aspects of Nursing*. Prentice Hall, London.

Dunstan G R and Seller M J 1983. *Consent in Medicine*. King Edward's Hospital Fund, London.

Farndale W A J 1981. *Aspects of Health Service Law*. Ravenswood, Beckenham.

Finch J D 1981. *Health Services Law*. Sweet & Maxwell, London.

Finch J D 1984. *Aspects of Law Affecting Paramedical Professions*. Faber & Faber, London.

Freeman M D A (ed.) 1988. *Medicine, Ethics and the Law: Current Legal Problems*. Stevens and Sons, London.

Gostin L 1983. *A Practical Guide to Mental Health Law*. MIND, London.

Grimes R 1986. *Law and the Elderly*. Croom Helm, London.

Harris J 1985. *The Values of Life*. Routledge & Kegan Paul, London.

Health Visitors Association 1983. *The Law and Health Visitors*. Esdall, London.

Hodgson J 1992. *Employment Law for Nurses*. Quay Publishing, Lancaster.

Hoggett B 1984. *Mental Health Law*, 2nd edition. Sweet & Maxwell, London.

Hoggett B 1987. *Parents and Children: the Law of Parental Responsibility.* Sweet & Maxwell, London.

Kennedy I and Grubb A 1989. *Medical Law and Ethics.* Butterworth, London.

Kennedy I 1991. *Treat me Right: Essays in Medical Law and Ethics.* Oxford University Press, Oxford.

Knight B 1982. *Legal Aspects of Medical Practice*, 3rd edition. Churchill Livingstone, Edinburgh.

Law B 1984. *Uses and Abuses of Profiling.* Harper & Row, London.

Leahy Taylor J 1982. *The Doctor and the Law*, 2nd edition. Pitman, London.

Lockwood M (ed.) 1985. *Moral Dilemmas in Modern Medicine.* Oxford University Press, Oxford.

Meyers D W 1970. *The Human Body and the Law.* Edinburgh University Press, Edinburgh.

Phillips M and Dawson J 1985. *Doctors' Dilemmas.* Harvester Press, Brighton.

Articles

Alderson P 1991. Out of the darkness. *Health Service Journal* 101, 3 October, pp. 22–24.

Alderson P 1992. In the genes or in the stars? Children's competence to consent. *Journal of Medical Ethics* **18**(3), pp. 119–124.

Andrews J 1989. Sneak or saviour (reporting bad practice of colleagues). *Nursing Times* **85**(9) p. 24.

Bowles R and Jones P 1990. Medical negligence and resource allocation in the NHS. *Social Policy Administration* **24**(1), pp. 29–51.

Carson D 1989. The case for advocates. *Health Service Journal* **99**, 9 March, pp. 298–9.

Cook A 1992. Squaring the circle. *Nursing Standard* **6**, 12 February, p. 46.

Cook T 1992. The nurse and informed consent. *Senior Nurse* **12**(2), March/April, pp. 41–45.

Crump A 1991. Your uninformed consent. *Nursing Standard* **5**, 13 March, pp. 22–24.

Deutsch E 1989. The right to be treated or to refuse treatment. *Medicine and Law* **7**(5), pp. 433–5.

Dimond B 1991. Accident, negligence or crime? *Nursing Standard* **5**, 13 February, pp. 22–24.

Fenner K M 1988. Nursing shortage; harbinger of increased litigation. *Nursing Management* **19**(11), pp. 44–45.

Gillon R 1989. Medical treatment, medical research and informed consent. *Journal of Medical Ethics* **15**(1), pp. 3–5, 11.

Herbert E 1989. Focus on COSHH, the practicalities. *Occupational Safety and Health* **19**(2), pp. 36–38.

Holmes G 1991. Are you really covered? *Practice Nursing*, May, pp. 8–9.

Howard G 1991. Pre-employment medicals and informed consent. *Occupational Health* **43**(8), August, pp. 241–242.

Kerrigan D D 1993. Who's afraid of informed consent? *British Medical Journal* **306**, 30 January, pp. 298–300.

Klop P 1991. Patients' rights and the admission and discharge process. *Journal of Advanced Nursing* **16**(4), April, pp. 408–412.

Johnstone M 1989. Law, professional ethics and the problems of conflict with personal values. *International Nursing Review* **36**(3), pp. 83–89.

Jones L 1989. Cruelty and neglect. *Nursing Times* **85**(4), pp. 52–54.

Lancet 1991. Informed consent: how informed? *Lancet* **388**, 14 September, pp. 665–666.

Letts P 1992. Consent to treatment – should the courts intervene? *Community Living* **6**(2), October, pp. 20–21.

MacFadyen J A 1989. Who will speak for me? Patient advocates in psychiatry. *Nursing Times* **85**(6), pp. 45–48.

Nicholson R 1990. Will new consent forms improve the quality of consent? *THS Health Summary* **7**(12), December, p. 4.

Parker S 1992. A changing culture. *Practice Nursing*, July/August, pp. 13–14.

Pinfold C 1991. Patient consent. *Senior Nurse* **11**(5), September/October, pp. 25–27.

Pope N 1989. Against the grain – anonymous testing for HIV. *Nursing Times* **85**(1), p. 19.

Pownall M 1989. When care has to be rationed: ethical issues. *Nursing Times* **85**(5), pp. 16–17.

Silverman W A 1989. The myth of informed consent: in daily practice and in clinical trials. *Journal of Medical Ethics* **15**(1), pp. 6–11.

Simanowitz A 1990. A fresh start. *Health Service Journal* **100**, 29 March, p. 470.

Tingle J H 1988. Nurses and the law. *Senior Nurse* **8** (1), January, pp. 8–10.

Tingle J H 1988. Some recent court cases of interest to nurses. *Senior Nurses* **8** (6), June, p. 11.

Tingle J 1990. The important case of Bull. *Nursing Standard* **4**, 6 June, pp. 54–55.

Tingle J 1990. A duty of care. *Nursing Times* **86**, 25 July, pp. 60–61.

Tingle J 1990. Patient consent – the issues. *Nursing Standard* **5**, 21 November, pp. 52–54.

Tingle J 1991. A hard lesson. *Nursing Times* **87**, 27 February, pp. 44–45.

Tingle J 1991. Negligence: the new accountability. *Nursing Standard* **5**, 10 April, pp. 18–19.

Tingle J 1992. Court in the slips. *Health Service Journal* **102**, 9 January, pp. 20–21.

Trainor J 1992. Action urged on clinical negligence claims. *Health Direct*, 24 November, p. 3.

Vaughan B 1989. Autonomy and accountability. *Nursing Times* **85**(3), pp. 54–5.

Viens D C 1989. History of nursing's code of ethics. *Nursing Outlook* **37**(1), pp. 45–49.

Vousden M 1989. Pressure points – professional misconduct. *Nursing Times* **85**(25), p. 48.

Whittington R and Wykes T 1992. Staff strain and social support in a psychiatric hospital following assault by a patient. *Journal of Advanced Nursing* **17**(4) April, pp. 450–486.

Wicker O P 1990. Legal responsibility of the nurse. 2 Negligence. *Surgical Nurse* **3**(6), December, pp. 20–22.

Wilson-Barnett J 1989. Limited autonomy and partnership: professional relationships in health care. *Journal of Medical Ethics* **15**(1), pp. 12–16.

Woodyard J 1990. Facing up to errors. *Health Service Journal* **100**, 29 March, pp. 468–469.

Useful Addresses

ALAS (Action for the Victims of Medical Accidents)
24 Southwark Street, London, SE1 1TY
(071–242 2430)

Advertising Standards Authority
Brook House, 2–16 Torrington Place, London, WC1E 7HN
(071–580 5555)

Age Concern
England   54 Knatchbull Road, London, SE5 9QY
(071–274 6723)
Northern Ireland   6 Lower Crescent, Belfast, BT7 1NR
(0232 245729)
Scotland   33 Castle Street, Edinburgh, EH2 4DN
(031–228 5656)
Wales   1 Park Grove, Cardiff, CF2 2YF
(0222 371821)

Amnesty International
99 Roseberry Avenue, London, EC1R 4RE
(071–278 6000)

Association of Community Health Councils for England and
Wales
30 Drayton Park, London, N5 1PB
(071–609 8405)

Association of Scottish Health Councils
21 Torpichen Street, Edinburgh, EH3 8HX
(031–229 2344)

British Geriatric Society
1 St Andrew's Place, London, NW1 4LB
(071–935 4004)

British Paediatric Association
  5 St Andrew's Place, London, NW1 4LB
  (071–486 6151)

Commission for Racial Equality
  Elliott House, 10–12 Allington Street, London, SW1 5EH
  (071–828 7022)

Confederation of Health Service Employees (COHSE)
  Glen House, High Street, Banstead, Surrey, SM7 2LH
  (07373 53322)

Court of Protection
  24 Kingsway, London, WC2
  (071–269 7000)

Department of Health
  Richmond House, 79 Whitehall, London, SW1
  (071–210 5983)

Department of Social Security
  Richmond House, 79 Whitehall, London, SW1
  (071–210 3000)

English National Board for Nursing, Midwifery and Health
  Visiting
  Victory House, 170 Tottenham Court Road, London, W1P 0HA
  (071–388 9244)

Equal Opportunities Commission
  Overseas House, Quay Street, Manchester, M3 3HN
  (061–833 9244)

Health and Safety Executive
  Baynard's House, 1 Chepstow Place, London, W2 4TF
  (071–221 0870)

Health Service Commissioner
  Church House, Great Smith Street, London, SW1P 3BW
  (071–276 3000)

Her Majesty's Stationery Office (HMSO)
  England 7 Trinity Street, London, SE1 1DA
  (071–378 6741)

Northern Ireland   80 Chichester Street, Belfast, BT1 4YJ
(0232 234488)
Scotland   71 Lothian Road, Edinburgh, EH3 9AZ
(031–479 9000)

HMSO Publications Centre
51 Nine Elms Lane, London, SW8 5DR

Industrial Tribunals – Central Office
93 Ebury Bridge Road, London, SW1W 8RE
(071–730 9161)

Justice
95A Chancery Lane, London, WC2A 1DT
(071–405 6018)

King's Fund Centre
126 Albert Street, London, NW2 7NF
(071–267 6111)

Law Centres Federation
Duchess House, Warren Street, London, W1P 5DA
(071–387 8570)

Law Commission
Conquest House, 37 John Street, London, WC1N 2AT
(071–242 0861)

Law Society
113 Chancery Lane, London, WC2A 1PL
(071–242 1222)

Law Society of Northern Ireland
Chichester Street, Belfast, BT2
(0232 231614)

Law Society of Scotland
26–27 Drumsheugh Gardens, Edinburgh
(031–226 7411)

Mental Health Act Commission
Room 22, Hepburn House, Marsham Street, London,
SW2P 4HW
(071–217 6016)

MIND (see National Association for Mental Health)

National Association of Citizen's Advice Bureaux
115 Pentonville Road, London, N1 9LZ
(071–833 2181)

National Association for Mental Health (MIND)
22 Harley Street, London, W1N 2ED
(071–637 0741)

National Board for Nursing, Midwifery and Health Visiting for
Northern Ireland
RAC House, 79 Chichester Street, Belfast, BT1 4JE
(0232 238152)

National Board for Nursing, Midwifery and Health Visiting for
Scotland
22 Queen Street, Edinburgh, EH2 1JX
(031–226 7371)

National Council for Civil Liberties (NCCL)
21 Tabard Street, London, SE2 4LA
(071–403 3888)

National Society for the Prevention of Cruelty to Children
(NSPCC)
67 Saffron Hill, London, EC1N 8RS
(071–242 1626)

National Union of Public Employees (NUPE)
8 Aberdeen Terrace, London, SE3 0QY
(081–852 2842)

Northern Ireland Civil Rights Association
2 Marquis Street, Belfast

Nurses Welfare Service
16–18 Strutton Ground, London, SW1P 2HP
(071–222 1563)

Patients' Association
18 Victoria Square, London, E2 9PF
(081–981 5676)

Police Federation
15–17 Langley Road, Surbiton, Surrey
(081–399 2224)

Royal College of Midwives
15 Mansfield Street, London, W1M 0BE
(071–580 6523)

Royal College of Nursing
20 Cavendish Square, London, W1M 0AB
(071–409 3333)

Trades Union Congress
Congress House, 23–28 Great Russell Street, London, WC1B
3LS
(071–636 4030)

UNISON
PO Box 386, London, WC1H 9BR

United Kingdom Central Council
23 Portland Place, London, W1N 3AF
(071–637 7181)

Welsh National Board for Nursing, Midwifery and Health
Visiting
13th Floor, Pearl Assurance House, Greyfriars Road, Cardiff,
CF1 3RT
(0222 395535)

Index